NO FEARS, NO EXCUSES

NO FEARS, NO EXCUSES

What You Need to Do to Have a Great Career

LARRY SMITH

Mariner Books   Houghton Mifflin Harcourt

BOSTON   NEW YORK

First Mariner Books edition 2017
Copyright © 2016 by Larry Smith

For information about permission to reproduce selections from
this book, write to trade.permissions@hmhco.com or to Permissions,
Houghton Mifflin Harcourt Publishing Company, 3 Park Avenue,
19th Floor, New York, New York 10016.

www.hmhco.com

Library of Congress Cataloging-in-Publication Data
Title: No fears, no excuses : what you need to do to have a great career / Larry Smith.
Description: Boston : Houghton Mifflin Harcourt, 2016.
Identifiers: LCCN 2015037676 |
ISBN 9780544663336 (hardback) | ISBN 9780544663282 (ebook) |
ISBN 9780544947207 (pbk.)
Subjects: LCSH: Career development. | Vocational guidance. | BISAC: BUSINESS &
ECONOMICS / Careers / General. | BUSINESS & ECONOMICS / Motivational.
Classification: LCC HF5381 .S627 2016 | DDC 650.1 — dc23
LC record available at http://lccn.loc.gov/2015037676

Book design by Brian Moore

Printed in the United States of America
DOC 10 9 8 7 6 5 4 3 2
4500711805

This book is dedicated to my students. They have taught me so much and inspired me so often.

CONTENTS

INTRODUCTION

Passion is a word we use often when we talk about our love lives, but rarely when it comes to our work lives. When you feel passionate about your work, there is no great difference between the way you feel on Monday morning and the way you feel on Saturday morning. When you feel passionate about your work, your workplace is not a prison that is meant to encase you until you've earned your freedom, and your work is not a means to an end. When you feel passionate about your work, you do not set rigid boundaries between work time and personal time, because the work itself is personal. When you feel passionate about your work, your talent has room to stretch and to grow.

I believe that such passion in work is available to everyone, without exception. It may not be a simple matter to identify it and achieve it, but it is available nonetheless. And by the time you've finished this book, you will see how. Why am I so confident? Simply because I have watched many hundreds of people from many different backgrounds with many different goals achieve great success using a handful of straightforward techniques.

I work in the heart of a university, and I see such a great waste of talent all around me. I have been cursed to watch such waste for decades. Young men and women enter my life when they are just students, filled with energy and drive. They hope to undertake wondrous adventures. They have amazing ideas and penetrating insights, ideas I would never have had at their age. They can make a computer or a cello sing, they can intuit solutions to mathematical problems I cannot understand, they can spin a tale or design a cupboard no one has ever seen before. Theirs is — without a doubt — real talent.

Yet, theirs is also raw talent. It is often naive, incomplete, unrefined, and so chaotically slapped together that its effect is weakened. Talent is sometimes found in a disheveled seventeen-year-old; other times it's in the polished demeanor of a twenty-seven-year-old; sometimes it's in those who will be the first in their families to be educated beyond high school; other times it's in those whose families are better educated; sometimes it's in someone newly arrived in the country. But the talent is there nevertheless, should you care to look.

I care to look. And I watch, waiting for these talented individuals to set their chosen worlds afire with their vision and commitment.

Unfortunately, they then grow up. The grown-up world is where talent goes to die.

The grownups I meet, whether former students or not, have all too often been captured by our worker-bee culture. The rules are clear: do what you are told and you get paid; work to live on the weekend and dread Monday; look forward to retirement and hope you do not end up dreading that as well; expect that pleasure or satisfaction in the work is an uncommon bonus.

This epidemic of lowered expectations has taken many victims, prompting the ever-common phrase: *I had to get realistic*. Consider how many people end their day at a bar or the dinner table, complaining about the boss or the work, and how many sit in frustrated silence.

My concern has increased over the years, and it has even led me to record a TEDx talk at the University of Waterloo, where I'm an adjunct associate professor of economics and a career counselor. The talk was called, "Why You Will Fail to Have a Great Career." There was no intent to craft a dismal message; I just tried to tell the truth as I've experienced it, drawing on the more than 20,000 conversations I have had about career success. (Yes, I actually do count and log my conversations. I'm an economist—I love data.) The TEDx video repeated the common and routine excuses I have heard too many times. Perhaps, I thought, it would stir a few people into action.

But as it turned out, millions watched, and my concern deepened. The challenge of finding a great career was affecting more people than I had thought. Some watched the video because they felt they needed the tough love the title of the talk promised; others because they were sure the title was wrong and needed to figure out why. Either way, an amazing range of email messages arrived: grateful, heart-rending, angry, inquisitive, skeptical, desperate, and confused. They came from parents, teenagers, educators, senior citizens, university students, recent graduates, middle-aged professionals, PhDs, men and women. The emails came from Canada, the United States, Mexico, Britain, France, Denmark, Portugal, Russia, Croatia, Greece, Turkey, and India.

Some found inspiration in my words. Some found cause to object. Others invented more excuses. Many asked for more guidance. And I had to wonder whether I did indeed have more guidance to offer. Career—your life's work—is too important to speculate about what *might* be true or useful. I decided to respond with this book for three reasons.

First, in spite of all the obstacles, I have seen plenty of people from diverse backgrounds create great careers for themselves, careers that give them profound satisfaction and create meaningful impact on the world around them. These people are a credit to their communities and role models to their families. They are happy. So I know it is possible.

Second, I happen to be one of these happy people with a great career. I found my passion early in life when, as a kid, I felt my teachers weren't doing a good enough job. While other kids built forts in their backyards, I created my own miniature classroom, complete with imaginary students. So I knew I'd be a teacher. But what would I teach? A history instructor in high school had a collection of books about finance and economics. I started reading them and never really stopped. But that doesn't mean everything fell into place. After I finished graduate school, I worked as an economist, ultimately finding a secure, stimulating job working for the Canadian government. There was room for growth, I enjoyed the people I worked with, and I had an opportunity to make real impact on public policy.

In short, it was a good job, but it wasn't a great career for me. I wanted to start my own consulting business, where I'd have more freedom to pursue my many areas of interest, from physics to architecture. I knew what I wanted, and yet my letter of resignation still sat on my desk for a week before I turned it in. I am afraid to think what I would have missed if I hadn't gone through with it.

That's not to say that everything has been simple from the day I decided to pursue a great career. My very first client as a consultant turned out to be a crook who fled the country one step ahead of the Royal Canadian Mounted Police. I was financially stressed, embarrassed, and my confidence took a hit. I didn't see that I had any choice but to keep my head down and keep working. I couldn't go back, so it was clear my only choice was to move forward. And I did.

After a while, I was ready to bring my love of teaching into the mix. Years earlier, professors and other advisors in my life told me I'd have to choose: economic research in the private sector or university teaching. I could delay the choice, of course, but ultimately I'd have to choose just one. This advice was well intentioned, but I decided to challenge it. It didn't make sense to me: *If you like to do multiple things,* I thought, *why wouldn't you?* I began to experiment, teaching just one course in Economics at University of Waterloo, and thirty years later, my teaching life is as active as my consulting business.

With teaching and economics firmly part of my work, it was time to incorporate a third passion: technology. I grew up on a farm in the country and, like most children, was fascinated by the farm machinery that seemed (and probably was) one hundred times bigger than me. My grandfather had used a flail to separate wheat from chaff, which is about as archaic a farming tool as you can imagine. But then came the reaping machine. And then the tractor and then the combine. Machinery, and the pace of technology, did not cease to amaze me as I grew older. I began to advise students about their startup tech companies and outside clients about their own work with emerging technologies. I can't write code, yet I get to help move such fields as robotics forward by advising companies on their marketing strategies.

I'd go crazy if I didn't have a plan to keep my life organized, and putting plans in place is something you will hear a lot about in this book. It's crucial. But so is passion. Because it is an amazing feeling when you don't really care if it's a weekend or not; it's so energizing to look forward to your work and not even think about retirement — why would you? The way I feel about my career is available to everyone, if only they know where and how to look.

Let me make clear what I mean by *passion*. A passion is more than an interest, although a passion may first appear as an interest. An interesting idea is easy to think about; when you have an idea that evokes passion, you cannot *stop* thinking about it. When you find a domain that engages passion, you want to understand it totally; you naturally see gaps that should be filled, errors that should be corrected, and innovations that cry out for creation. With passion, there is an inherent tendency to take action. None of those elements is necessarily present when you find something "interesting."

Passion invites an intensity of enduring focus. Interests, by contrast, ebb and flow and sometimes vanish. Yes, passion also evolves as we gain experience; it may broaden or deepen, or stretch into adjacent areas. And you may, of course, have more than one passion, or you may discover a new one. With passion, you have the wind at your back, just as I have for so many years.

But the final reason I wanted to write this book is perhaps the most critical. I am in a unique position to draw on the experiences of the thousands of people I have advised about careers. Indeed, I have collected 30,000 career statements over the years. You should know something about the University of Waterloo, too: It is a unique environment, with an unparalleled co-op program, the largest in the world. This means that more than 19,000 of our students will devote alternate semesters of their education to gainful employment. We have more than 6,000 active employers who visit campus and hire our students for degree-related jobs. Our students get real-life work experience, even as they are pursuing their degrees.

You can see, I think, why career conversations at Waterloo tend to be very robust? My students work at Goldman Sachs, Microsoft, in Hollywood, and at small startups in the United States, Canada, and Asia. You would be hard-pressed to name a midsize or large company in North America where a student of mine hasn't worked. My students, who come from many diverse backgrounds, ask for my advice when they're nineteen, and they return to my doorstep at thirty to report on their progress. In some cases, they didn't take my advice when younger but now feel ready. When you consider that I've been at this for thirty years, you realize that what I have is, in effect, a thorough, long-term study.

This book is therefore not a recipe concocted from the idiosyncratic pathway of an individual, celebrity or otherwise. Rather, it's driven by a weight of evidence that some career strategies work and others don't. These strategies have been applied to almost every kind of career, from the skilled trades to the work of PhDs to creative endeavors. They have been used by those young and old, shy and loud, nervous and confident.

You will read many stories in this book about my students and those I have advised. Some have agreed to be identified by their real names. For the others, to protect their confidentiality, I have disguised their attributes, changed some portions of their stories, and, in some cases, created composites of several students. While I have opted to give the students popular names like "John" and "Trent," it should be noted that many of those featured in this book come from diverse populations. I opted for overly common names in order to prevent perpetuating stereotypes or inadvertently allowing any student to be recognized. Nevertheless, every strategy discussed in this book has been validated in actual employment situations.

The approach of this book is straightforward. It offers the evidence of experience, organized in response to the most common questions arising from the TED correspondence. The book will address such questions as the following: Isn't a great career just a bonus? Don't most people just learn to "love" their work? How can I find passion? How can I reconcile the pursuit of a great career with family responsibilities? How can I find a great career if I'm not special? What if my passion doesn't afford a livelihood? How can I overcome my fear of failure? Isn't money enough to make a career "great"? What really makes a career "great"?

The answers strive to be realistic. They are neither easy nor magical. They acknowledge that you live in a world hostile to the realization of talent. But a great career is within your grasp, if you choose to learn from the experiences of those who have already succeeded.

To ensure that you have fully grasped the message of a chapter, I'll ask you several questions at the end of each one. Please think about these questions and answer them honestly — they'll help you prepare for the chapters that follow. By the end of the book, you will understand what you need to do to have a great career, and why you need to do it.

I must warn you — it won't always be comfortable to read what I have to say. My purpose isn't to put you to sleep with soft words, but to wake you up. As Vitor, a gentleman from Portugal, wrote after he heard me speak on the matter, "I considered [your speech] disruptive, extremely uncomfortable to listen to, acutely offensive, and . . . an incredibly accurate depiction of my whole life so far."

It's my intention to fully disrupt you — to get you to throw your old-fashioned notions and 1980s strategies out the window. Because a great career is essential. And a great career is yours for the taking.

Larry Smith
Fall, 2015

PART I

FINDING YOUR PASSION

ONE

Why Good Work Is No Longer Good Enough

JOHN WAS SURE his life was on track. Upon graduation, a degree in computer science in hand, he had joined one of the world's great and iconic IT firms. They paid well, with generous benefits, and after five years of good performance reviews, he had been promoted to team manager. John was married, lived in a large house in an upscale neighborhood, and he and his spouse were talking about children. John had even begun making contributions to a retirement account.

Charlene's life was in sharp contrast to John's. Though she excelled in science and math in high school, she chose to study sociology because it was "about people" and math "bored" her. Upon her college graduation, the only job she was offered was at a call center. When she was told that if she worked there for five years, she might be promoted to be the team leader, she declined the position and went back to graduate school to continue her studies in sociology. "When in doubt, go to school," had been her motto. Nearing her second graduation, Charlene found that her employment options included high school teacher, and little else. (Ideally she would have researched this much earlier on, but more on that later.) Charlene may not have been sure what she wanted, exactly, but she knew with certainty that she did not want to be a high school teacher. To buy time, Charlene took a clerical job, filing and fetching.

Today one of these people has upward momentum, financial success, and security; the other is stalled, with few opportunities for improvement. One is confident; one is apprehensive. Perhaps you think you already know which is which. But you are wrong if you think Charlene is the one who is doomed to struggle.

Why John Struggled: Competition and the Demise of the 9-to-5er

If this had been 1980, John's comfortable world would have been assured. But he was born too late. When his general manager asked to see him one day, John had no idea he was at risk. Indeed, it took a few minutes before John recognized he was being terminated.

It made no sense. His company was growing and profitable; his performance reviews were favorable; he had done nothing wrong. The manager was vague, citing changing corporate priorities, and talked about severance. John was still numb when he read in the news media the following day that his employer had laid off hundreds of employees because their skills were deemed inadequate. Now John was mystified; he'd never failed at any task he was given, so how could he be judged to be deficient?

Actually, there was little mystery about why John found himself in this difficult position. He'd been sucker-punched by outside competition and kicked in the head by technology. The warning signs had long been there, had John cared to notice them. For several years, the business media had covered his employer unfavorably. There was much commentary about the company missing recent new developments in IT, while other companies advanced on its markets. It was criticized for losing its competitive edge. In my conversation with John it was clear that he had paid no attention to these concerns and was barely aware of them. "We're still profitable," he noted, correctly. (And I noted he was still saying "we" when, in fact, he was no longer part of the team.) John went on to insist that since the company was profitable, the media criticism was unfair.

"Could it be," I suggested, "that the company has finally concluded that the critique is valid? That future profitability is at risk?"

"Maybe," he said. "But it still doesn't make sense. If they're concerned about competition, why fire me, when I have tons of experience and always get my work done, and hire newer, less-experienced people?"

In the media coverage about the terminations, there had been references to the company getting rid of the "9-to-5ers." I asked John if this description might have applied to him, and he said he didn't even know what it meant. It was time to get blunt; only truth would serve John now. So I told him that the term was dismissive, implying that the 9-to-5er just puts in his time doing ordinary work, instead of aggressively using initiative to tackle whatever problem appears to be important.

"The company doesn't like that," John said firmly, referring to the aggressive initiator. But maybe that had changed. Maybe some of the executives were 9-to-5ers, and they were gone, too.

"John," I said, "do you recognize that, by several measures, your former employer is losing to other, more nimble competitors?"

John's answer was "Maybe," indicating that he didn't see it. He had unfortunately taken his job for granted. He had chosen computing as a career because it was in such high demand. And having chosen computing, he'd figured there was nothing else to worry about. He would work as long as he chose. But look at all the evidence he had ignored. Is it evidence you are also ignoring?

How could he — or you — discount the fact that, for much of the last sixty years, if you were a large and market-dominant company, you could expect to reign for decades? If you were General Motors, IBM, Sears, Kodak, U.S. Steel, Polaroid, or Xerox, it would have been suicidal for competitors to attack you. And then, more swiftly than might have been imagined, Japanese imports suddenly destabilized the auto market of the former Big Three. IBM was blindsided by Microsoft and Intel. Technological advances pushed Kodak, Xerox, and Polaroid to the sidelines. Apple disrupted the established music industry, even as Uber destabilized the taxi/limo business. And these examples barely skim the surface.

Here's what happened next: Microsoft suddenly faced competition from cloud computing and mobile devices. Google quickly found itself under pressure from Facebook, which was itself under pressure from instant messaging services. If you don't grasp just how quickly this all happened, then you don't understand how gentle the past was. Dominance was supposed to last many decades, not just a few decades or even sometimes just one. Most of this disruption happened in John's lifetime, and even a superficial knowledge of the past would have helped him see the future.

Please understand, I was not trying to make John feel badly about himself. He felt terrible enough already, and his self-confidence was seriously damaged. His confidence hadn't collapsed yet, but I feared it would when he started his job search. The conversation with John was painful, and I have had more than one such conversation. Many more than one.

You can see, I think, why I decided it would be wrong to tell him about Charlene's success. He wasn't yet ready to hear about it.

Why Charlene Thrived: Change and the Ever-Demanding Consumer

Charlene had needed no one to tell her about the force of competition. She knew that if she was going to get a job as a sociologist that did not involve teaching, she'd face intense competition. Or do you think a sociology major should take *any* half-decent job offered? You can imagine Charlene's anxious parents having that point of view, encouraging her to grasp at the low-hanging fruit. They may have been eager for her to use her major and start on a path to repaying her loans — what could be wrong with that? But Charlene had ambition; she wanted a great job, a great career. And so she focused on both her goal and the means to achieve it.

Charlene found the history of social change fascinating. *All* of it was interesting to her; technical change interested her as much as shifts in cultural norms. In spite of the fact that she couldn't write a line of code, she understood the transformative force of computing and its social and commercial potential far better than John had. That gave her the first step in her job search. If change was her primary interest, then she should gravitate toward the source of greatest visible change: the tech sector.

For Charlene it was obvious that the consumer was becoming ever more demanding, wanting better products, not just more of them. Now quality was as desirable as quantity. It used to be that people were simply happy to have food. No longer — food must be fresh, free of pesticides, locally raised, ecologically harvested, and 1 percent of the profit must support charity. And in the quieter past, a car was a car. But competition told consumers they could demand cars that lasted longer, so warrantees lengthened. Then they wanted cars that came with roadside assistance. Then the cars had to be capable of parking themselves . . . and so it goes for all products and services. Phones are no longer permitted to be dumb; they must be able to hear and speak, tell us where we need to go and how to get there; they must entertain us and reheat our afternoon snack. And never, ever must our products bore us. Oh, and even with all of this, we expect our products to be easily affordable.

Charlene saw change through this wider lens, but in truth, most of my students do not. If you text, sext, tweet, browse, surf, and selfie, it's easy to believe you are a master of technology. But really, all that means is that you're a master of today's technology — what about yesterday's? Understanding what used to be is critical for grasping technology's impact and pace. Looking back to understand the way forward was in fact Charlene's specialty.

Action vs. Reaction

Charlene never saw a job posting for what she wanted to do, so there was no other choice but to wait until . . . No, wait — that's yesterday's response.

Here's what Charlene did instead: she took action. Charlene began to write about technological change and the consumer, posting blogs wherever her techie friends suggested. A few unpaid magazine articles followed. Charlene haunted tech networking events. Finally, a small firm that was told that their marketing materials lacked "punch" hired her part-time to give them "something cool" to say. Charlene gave them an almost poetic description of their product that whet consumers' appetites.

What was John doing while Charlene was laying the groundwork for a great career? He was reacting. At his former job, he'd spent his time writing code, laying the groundwork to write even more code. Now that he was no longer employed, he still wasn't concerned enough to take action — he was still in reaction mode. What had happened to him, he felt, was an unfair bump in the road, but since he was an IT guy, another job should be reasonably easy to get. It would take a couple of months at most, he thought, and his spouse and savings would keep them afloat until he started working again.

But then it got complicated. They couldn't afford to put his wife's job at risk, so moving to another city did not seem wise in the short term. Excluding his employer, there weren't many large IT firms in the area. He approached them all, some of whom were on record as complaining about IT shortages in the tech sector.

John got interviews, but as it turned out, the firms were looking for newer specializations, like cloud computing and deep-data mining. John pointed out that his skills were broad-based and he could learn whatever specialties he needed. While the interviewers nodded and said they would keep him in mind, John was acutely aware that in the reception lobby, a number of younger, just-graduated faces waited for their turn to interview. John reassured himself, figuring that even if those new graduates had taken courses in cloud computing, they didn't have his depth of experience.

Too bad it wasn't experience that mattered. Even worse, the reality of his termination hovered over the interview. Was he a 9-to-5er? If his big employer, who could carry some dead weight, didn't want him, why would a new employer take a chance on him?

Finally, John got a job offer at a small inventory software firm, at half his former salary. He had always judged his self-worth according to his income, and was devastated. But what choice did he have?

Charlene, meanwhile, had moved to a midsize tech firm, using her sociology background to help them craft their array of social media products. And here again, Charlene's education paid off.

She was never happier than when she was trying to understand why some cultural practices that had been around for centuries changed in just a generation. For instance, she obsessed over how women had entered the urban labor force in unprecedented numbers and in occupations in which they had previously been almost absent. She wanted to understand why corporate loyalty had diminished so quickly that the young did not even know it used to exist. It was a slow realization, but Charlene saw her interest in social change fit another great cultural change of its own: the growth in the importance of social media. Who better to understand and use it than Charlene? She saw the fortunes of history flowing toward her; John saw them ebbing away from him.

John's Reeducation

John returned to see me just as he was to take his 50 percent wage cut. He wanted some tips for networking to find something better. I suggested that what he really needed to do was a strategic rethink.

"No, I don't need that — I just have to get something that pays better," he said.

Finally, there was no choice but to openly tell him that his employment challenge was systemic. Unless he was prepared to address it, further conversation would be a waste of time. John looked very displeased, but he made no move to leave.

I needed to offer John some context, so I told him I'd spent much of my early childhood on a farm too remote for electricity, where entertainment was a battery-operated radio, and where the telephone was a party line shared with another dozen families. There was no running water and my mother and grandmother cooked on a wood stove. John looked as surprised as if I had told him I was a Martian.

"When I was a kid," I continued, "cars froze up in the winter, and long-distance calls were so expensive they were made only for emergencies. Television, jet airplanes, mainframe computers, personal computers, organ transplants, genetic engineering, DNA testing, in-vitro fertilization, computer animation, and the Internet *arrived* in my lifetime. But why do you think I'm telling you this?"

"So I'll know you've seen lots of change?" John suggested.

"No," I said. "I'm telling you this because you will see *even greater* changes."

The workforce has changed just as dramatically, and I explained this to John, too. In my youth, I had my choice of "good" jobs. A simple interview got you an offer, since the interviewer was really just interested in whether there was something obviously wrong with you. You were offered adequate pay, a job for life unless you were a total screw-up, and you retired with a defined-benefits plan that guaranteed your income. Financial markets were quiet and predictable, so all you had to do was save and you had an easily assured way to build some additional wealth.

Typical jobs now involve wages that barely rise, workloads that leave nothing but the scraps of a personal life, and stress that grows daily. The odds of finding a "good" career are fading fast — and all because of economic competition.

Since I'm an economist, I reminded John, I naturally think about competition quite a lot. Competitive pressures keep rising, and they aren't going to stop in this century. The number of competing countries, companies, and workers continues to increase. If by some miracle the number of competitors were to stop rising, technological change would continue. A single technical change could disrupt an entire industry and quickly disadvantage its existing companies and employees. The truth is that competition and technology are dancing together to an ever-faster beat; John had no choice but to dance along, and you have no choice, either.

A New Strategy

Even though the duo of competition and technology is a defining characteristic of our age, much commented upon, people don't really do anything about it. It doesn't affect the way they think, or the way they approach their careers. For John and many others, competition, technology, and the blistering pace of change are no more than words spoken casually in a bar.

Now it was time to tell John about Charlene.

I explained her background and noted that she had just been hired for a high-profile job with a rapidly expanding social media company. Predictably enough, John asked if I was recommending that he try to get a job in social media.

"Do you find social media fascinating?" I asked.

"Not exactly . . . no."

"And with neither relevant education nor experience, could you compete with Charlene and those like her?"

"Well, no," he replied.

"Exactly. I'm not recommending Charlene's particular *choice* for you, but her *strategy*."

For the first time since he'd entered my office that day, John smiled. At last, he was ready to talk about career strategy.

We began with a review of what doesn't work, which covered most of the things most people actually do. The kinds of career plans I see would do justice to John's grandparents. Most people just do what everyone else with the same job in mind does: get the same education, acquire the same skills, build the same résumé, and provide the same answers to interview questions.

The strategy most often employed is this: Get an education. More competition? Get more education. More competition? Get some relevant experience. More competition? Get even more experience. But everyone else is adding experience at the same rate. Believing you can advance your career solely by celebrating another birthday does not seem a very sophisticated strategy for the twenty-first century.

I asked John what the flaw of this approach was. He understood that the primary problem was that almost everyone else was doing it. The only way it could work is if you outlasted everyone: Career by endurance.

"Think about the consequences," I said. "As the situation becomes ever more competitive, you make yourself like everyone else? In what world would that make sense? You've essentially made yourself into a commodity, and one that's interchangeable. And the commodity worker is bid down to the lowest price possible."

John now saw where his wage cut came from. "I definitely don't want to be a commodity," John said emphatically.

"Great," I replied. "Let's talk about how you become a star."

Before we got into the details of a better career strategy, John first needed to understand his destination: Not a job, not a good job, not even a great job. He should aim instead for a great career.

A career is great when it offers satisfying work, impact on the world, a dependable and adequate income, and personal freedom.

If John had a great career, defined in this way, he wouldn't have to worry about being fired. If he was using his skills in the service of work that was satisfying and meaningful to him, he would not be a replaceable cog or commodity, but an exceptional asset whose contributions could not be replicated. He would have an edge.

True, you don't become a star like this quickly. But you will never become a star if you don't even know that's your objective, or if every aspect of your career plan isn't focused on becoming exceptional.

So what would John do to create edge? While I will discuss what people like John need to do in the following chapters, it all begins with one simple question: Can you create any significant degree of credible edge without a passionate interest in the work itself? Can you imagine creating this edge, this commanding competitive advantage that will survive your working life, *without* such passion? How could you bring the intensity of purpose and commitment that is necessary without passion? How will you compete with those who have real passion?

Jake's Jobs: A Choose-Your-Own Adventure

Let me tell you a story about my good friend Jake, because you need to embark on your career journey with a healthy dose of reality, but an equally healthy dose of vision.

Jake loves his work, and his employer loves him. He is so valuable an employee that Jake has job security for as long as he'd like to keep the job.

But his career didn't start out that way. Indeed, at one time, it looked like Jake would be roadkill, collateral damage in the brutal labor markets of the twenty-first century.

No matter what Jake had tried in his career, it hadn't worked out. After college graduation, he got an excellent job at a multi-billion-dollar telecommunications company. It wasn't that he loved the job or the field of telecommunications. Rather, the job paid well, it was available, and the seemingly stable company was willing to train him. What's to think about? So he didn't think. He just took it, and started down a path. (Sounds a little like John, doesn't he?)

Jake built up his experience and underwent extensive training in emerging new communications technology. He even fell under the protection of a powerful union. He was seemingly set for life.

Unfortunately, under the pressure of rapidly changing technology and fleet-footed competitors, Jake's employer stumbled and then crashed, taking Jake along with it. Since the entire telecom industry was in upheaval, no one was hiring. So Jake's experience was of no immediate value, and the technology was moving so quickly that his experience soon became obsolete. What to do?

Jake was no quitter. He took stock of his transferable skills and landed a job in logistics in the packaged-goods industry. This time, the pay wasn't as good, but it was a decent job with security. We'll always need logistics, right? Well, no, not exactly. With an economic slowdown and rising competitive pressure, the packaged goods industry went through a bout of consolidation, and Jake was unemployed again.

Jake took a couple of junk day jobs, one as a loading-dock laborer, another as a furniture mover, as he upgraded his computer skills. Using the standard career playbook, Jake networked and applied relentlessly. Then he scored a job as logistics manager for a North American manufacturer with a quality product in high demand. Finally, Jake was sure his career was back on track.

Barely a year after Jake started, Chinese manufacturers discovered the product category and entered with a much lower price.

Jake's company collapsed over the next two years, leaving Jake looking for work yet again.

Jake was in a race with both technology and competition, and each time he was ahead, he got slapped down. He felt like there was a monster following him.

I can only imagine the pressure he felt as his family's primary breadwinner. From his highest salary, his income had eroded by *more than a third*. There were two paths before him.

In Path #1, Jake says, "Screw this. I'm done trying." He puts his head down. "I'll just be an administrative assistant or something, and accept that I'll never own a house or a car, or be able to afford an indulgence like a motorcycle. I'll be careful with money, give everything I earn to my kids' welfare, and we'll somehow be okay." In other words, he capitulates to competition. What kind of life would that be? Grayer than gray. And yet I see so many people choosing Path #1. Path #1 makes me twitch.

I'm pleased to say that Jake followed Path #2. Jake was smart and thoughtful, and, even more importantly, he wasn't a quitter. First, he thought he'd look for an industry where there wasn't competition. It wouldn't be glamorous, but it would be safe. But then he noticed something. You see, his job situation meant that he was spending a lot more time at home during this period, and seeing his kids a lot. He watched the way his nine-year-old daughter was fearless. She tried *everything*, from kickboxing to gymnastics to debate to science decathlons. She failed at some of them, but she shrugged it off and moved on. She was intrepid and she was resilient. Jake wondered what message he would be sending her if he just retreated to "safe."

More than his daughter's influence, though, Jake came to realize that there was no place to hide from competition. In every area he explored, he saw that even if it was a safe zone now, there was nothing to suggest it would remain so — he knew that better than most. As long as he was running away from competition, he realized, he was going to lose. Instead, he would run *toward* competition. He would make competition an asset instead of the monster constantly stalking him.

With this new mindset, he first asked himself, *What will always be important in a competitive market?* Salesmanship. Because as competition rises, you need someone who can sell better than the others.

Second, he wondered what he could sell. He was passionate about travel, though he hadn't been able to do it as much as he'd have liked. But how to sell travel? He remembered he and his wife had once sat in on a timeshare presentation, and he hadn't been able to stop thinking about how he'd have done it differently.

Once he had a handle on what he'd like to sell, he wondered what kind of timeshare salesperson he could be. He'd never sold before, but he knew he was a good "people person." He frequently received feedback that he was easy to talk to, which he attributed to the fact that he was genuinely interested in people. He was friendly and funny, and he looked people in the eye when he talked to them. He was the kind of person who was always asked to speak at weddings. All of this also meant he was a smooth networker — only it wasn't even networking, because he just naturally gravitated to new people and loved talking with them.

Finally, Jake needed to determine how he might get such a job. For one, he had a strong network of friends who might know someone who could help him enter the field. He also realized that sales is one of those relatively easy areas in which to prove yourself. Jake read voraciously to understand the travel and tourism market. Then he found someone willing to entertain the idea of hiring him and said, "Let me try, and judge me on my performance." He believed in himself, and so he set up a test. It was a brilliant strategy, and it worked. Jake's business is now mainly referrals from past customers, which, as any businessperson knows, are gold. He frequently travels to see areas his clients are particularly interested in, so that he can speak in an educated manner about those locales. He has developed a specialty for timeshares and second homes in the British Virgin Islands, an area of the world he loves. He is a top earner at his company, and even if the market falls, he will outlast most of the competition because he is just that good at what he does. And if he ever needs to, he knows he can always sell something else. For again, in a competitive market, there will always be salespeople.

Finally, Jake had work he enjoyed and a clear strategy to sustain his success. Charlene, too, was pursuing a passionate interest and was rewarded with career success. John, by contrast, was looking for no more than a job and was struggling as a result.

Jake does not appear again in this book, yet he is everywhere in this book. His is a classic "great career" success story, one that has absolutely nothing to do with luck and everything to do with an analytical approach, a methodical process, and determination. The rest of the book will show you how, while you might feel tempted to take Path #1, the path of least resistance, Path #2 leads to a great career.

One of my former students, Harout, wrote to me recently about some changes in his job, and I found in his email a timely comment to sum up the central message of chapter 1 and, indeed, of this book. "The company has been shifting to an outsourcing model for years," he wrote. "Soon only knowledgeable staff who review and evaluate outside tenders [proposals] will remain . . . I thought I had found a good job and a good career, but they're disappearing. Now, I will be forced to have a great one."

Hard Questions, Honest Answers

1. Look at the path you're on now. How did you get here? Was it because it was easy, or because it was where you wanted to be?

2. Are you a 9-to-5er? Might your boss believe you to be?

TWO

Why "Safe" Jobs Are a Myth

NOT LONG AGO, I attended a retirement celebration dinner for a good friend who was a judge. Though the environment was festive, there was also some sadness. You see, this friend loved his job. Many of the people attending the dinner also loved their jobs, and so they understood the mixed blessing that would come with retirement.

"What will he do without his work?" one friend sitting at my table asked, and I knew she meant it not in the "how will he fill his time?" respect, for he had plenty of exciting things lined up. But his love for his job was such that leaving it represented a real loss. Believe it or not, I try not to lecture everyone I meet. But since the subject was so applicable to the way I spend my days, I added, "I know — his passion for his work is remarkable. It's that kind of passion that I'm always telling my students they must pursue."

The woman sitting next to me, whom I did not know very well, became instantly offended. "That is terrible, dangerous advice," she said. "That's advice to leave kids unemployed." So swift and strong was her reaction that I understood she probably had a son or a daughter looking to find his or her way, perhaps living in the family basement while cobbling together shifts at the local pizza joint. No doubt she worried for her child, wanting more than anything to see her offspring become a self-supporting member of society.

I was not surprised to hear her argument, for it's a common one. Refrains I hear most often include: *Chasing passion is like chasing an unrealizable dream!* or *In this economy, there's no room for passion — it's all about skill. If you develop a skill, you'll love your work.* I had the good sense not to make our tablemates even more uncomfortable by thrusting them into the middle of a debate, and so I merely smiled at the woman next to me, suggested we saw passion differently, and changed the subject.

So, instead of speaking my mind that night, I saved everything I would have loved to say for this chapter. I can't anticipate every argument of my detractors, but there are a few I've heard enough to know by heart. I've included them here, as well as my responses. Informing all of my replies, of course, was the hard truth I laid out in chapter 1, that in this competitive economy, there is no "good" career. With that as my bass note, the arguments below take on the tinny sound of a single high note — easy to overpower.

Argument #1: Every passionate career needs a backup plan.

Part of why I did not come down too hard on my dinner companion was that I understood why she was upset. Parents want only the best for their kids. They do not want to see their children suffer or struggle with unemployment. I certainly wouldn't want that for my children or for any of the students I've advised. In other words, this mother and I were coming from the same place: one of love and a desire to protect our children.

But how to go about girding our children against hardship is where our approaches diverge dramatically. For instance, let's talk about the backup plan. Even those parents who entertain the idea of their children finding their passions are known to advise, *Go ahead and find your passion, but just be sure you have something to fall back on.* This refrain might be the most common one in the parental songbook. By "something," they mean a skill. And by skill, they probably mean something "safe" like dentistry or bookkeeping.

Again, this argument is perfectly understandable. Just as, when children are young, you suggest they bring a coat just in case the weather gets bad, when they're older, you also want them to be prepared.

But the backup plan is not equivalent to the extra layer of clothing on a temperamental spring day. The backup plan, you see, actually sets the individual back instead of protecting her or pushing her forward. It's a detour, and one that might take your youngster completely off course.

I had a debate on the matter with my student Henry, whose plan was to pursue his skill as a backup plan. In this case, the skill was cloud computing. His passion, however, was writing. Henry came to see me, frustrated, because he was trailing his computing classmates on the grade front.

"Are you passionate about the cloud, then?" I asked.

"I don't know. It's sort of interesting."

"Ah. And are you going to pursue your writing career while you're also pursuing your career in cloud computing? Or do you plan to pursue computing first, and then writing?" Again, Henry wasn't sure, but he was leaning toward the latter.

"Let me ask you something, Henry. How long do you plan to live, exactly?"

"Um . . . What?"

"We are talking about your LIFE, are we not?" I told him that his plan as he'd explained it to me could take a long time — a very long time. "And do you intend to put the rest of your life on hold in the meanwhile?"

"I don't understand," he said.

And so I walked him through it. I could see him pursuing his skill, cloud computing, and then getting a job using his skill. But then, when he decided he had his backup plan all well and established and was now ready to pursue his passion, writing, he might have to return to school to be trained for it. Would he really be prepared to do that? What if, in the meanwhile, he met someone he'd like to marry? Would he be willing to pursue marriage and his writing career at once? Would the lucky lady be open to him doing so? Assuming she gave him her blessing to take on student debt so he could chase his dreams, what would he do if they decided to have kids?

In short, while I don't actually believe you are ever too old to begin pursuing your passion, there's no denying that it's simpler and easier if you do so from the start. As people get older, life does get more complicated.

What happens to so many — and what I was certain would happen to Henry — is that the passion plan is tucked away, never to emerge again. Indeed, I feared Henry would be back in my office several years down the road, distressed and very possibly depressed because he took no satisfaction in his work and felt trapped by it.

The backup plan appears sensible, appears safe, and therein lies its great danger. The backup plan is the thick mud that lies between you and your true passions. You don't intend to get stuck there, and you're sure you'll only be stronger for having pushed through it. But you *do* get stuck. What was supposed to have given you security has only slowed your real progress.

I know this because of how often I see it. My student Allie began a graduate program in library science because she presumed she'd enjoy it. Once she'd enrolled, she felt stuck. She could tell from the first semester of classes that library school had been the wrong choice for her, but she remained. She explained, "Well, I started it. I needed to finish." When she graduated, she was qualified to work as a librarian, and she did so, even though she hated it.

Unfortunately, many people make the same choice: to pursue something solely because they started it. Indeed, that is the most common reason students give me when I ask why they finished something they had long known was not right for them.

A fellow named Brad learned this lesson the hard way and wrote to me about it. He explained that focusing first on security and money in the hopes that passion and happiness will come later in life makes finding happiness more complicated than it should be. "It's far inferior to taking a direct route to your passion and happiness," he wrote. "One thing I don't think enough people realize is that it's going to be much harder to find a passion if you never deviate from the same routine. Most people are such creatures of habit, and afraid to step out of their comfort zone, that they will never get the exposure to something new that *might* lead to a passion."

You see, then, that although the backup plan is filled with good intentions, it leads to unhappiness all too easily. A young woman named Sabrina who saw me speak on this subject wrote, "I chose the next part of my career based on a passion for stem cells that I have harbored and my father had nurtured since I was eight. Before watching your video, I was hesitant to pursue my choice as I felt compelled to apply to professional schools like dentistry and optometry like my peers, solely for job stability and economics, even though what a dull and boring life that would be for me. My father could have benefited from your speech 21 years ago, because he chose the economic route, and now he is paying for it. He routinely describes his career as a high workload, high-stress, blood-sucking, soul-destroying kind of job."

Reader, allow me to ask you this: Since we are protective of our children, why would we send them on a blood-sucking and soul-destroying path?

Argument #2: The current market demands high skills, not passion!

The argument seems quite clear: Pick a skill that is in demand and acquire it through education, training, and experience. We have to take this view seriously, because it is the view of the majority of people. (Passion advocates like myself can make a lot of noise, but those who put passion first are in the minority.) As I noted in chapter 1, competitive pressures have increased and will continue doing so, with the labor market becoming ever more challenging. Unskilled work is almost completely disappearing, transferred to the realm of robots. So of course skill seems like the way forward, and the more skill, the better.

But here's the problem with that argument: Many people focus on the competitiveness of today's labor market and pay no attention to what the market will look like fifteen years from now, never mind fifty years from now. Anytime I look at a young face, I *must* look to the next fifty years or I may as well keep my mouth shut completely, which I've never been particularly good at. And when you look at the next fifty years, you see, the "skills first!" argument makes little sense. Let's assume you look at skilled jobs where there's a lot of hiring going on, like high-tech or medicine. That should mean the skill is in growing demand and there will be a place for you when you complete your training, right? No, not at all. That approach has blown up in people's faces repeatedly, because what is "hot" now will not be so tomorrow. Consider these examples: A young man in high school is barely passing, so the school tells his parents he likes working with his hands and should learn a trade. He likes cars, so he chooses to be a car mechanic. There will always be cars to repair, right? He starts his training as an apprentice, and figures he's set for life. The young guy is so happy: cars, girls, and big bucks. He's on his way. Then the auto makers build cars to a much higher standard of quality, and relatively fewer repairs are needed. Electronics replace mechanical parts. The shortage of car mechanics suddenly disappears, if there ever was one. It's called the *advance of technology*.

It's the 1990s; the Internet is being built out *for the first time*. There's a shortage of telecommunications engineers, and the telecoms tell universities to expand their telecommunications degree programs as fast as possible or risk slowing the progress of the Internet. The telecom classes become packed. Then the Internet bust occurs. The telecoms overbuilt, and *overhired*. Telecommunications engineers everywhere are released to pursue opportunities elsewhere. They have wonderful résumés for telecom — and for nothing else.

They had bet on skill in a technology, and both the technology and the marketplace moved on. People said *Don't worry — just wait it out. The marketplace will improve. The Internet will continue expanding.* Yes, and that does happen, but it takes five years. Five years is a long time when you have a kid to support and a mortgage to pay. Plus, when things pick up again five years later, the telecom students of the late 1990s will be behind. The Internet has changed rapidly, and it's the new crop of telecom grads who get the new wave of jobs.

Generations have believed the job of high school teacher to be a safe, skilled choice. We'll always need teachers, right? No. In most of the industrial world, including the United States, the birth rate has fallen substantially and the population is slowing or starting to decline. This means that, in the absence of immigration, the number of children will decrease. And suddenly we will need fewer teachers because there are fewer children.

You get my point, I'm sure. The list of hot jobs, hot skills that suddenly grew cold is long indeed. Website designers were in short supply at first, and now a kid with software can whip up a credible site. Webmasters were replaced by social media masters, who will be replaced by something we don't even know about yet. As I write this, deep-data-mining specialists are in short supply. But for how long?

In the pursuit of safe, well-paying jobs, immigrant families in particular often herd their children into what they see as the best possible choice — a high-skill *regulated* profession. By this I mean physicians, lawyers, engineers, and accountants, all of whom must be licensed to practice, and all of whose work is essential. This route seems ideal to the immigrant parents who took substantial and personal risks to improve the lives of their children, who now are supposed to *take no risks at all*. Leaving aside the inconsistency of the approach (risk-taking parents who are surprised they raised risk-taking children), *all* the traditional professions are under siege by technology and global competition. Legal and accounting work gets either absorbed by software or outsourced to lower-wage countries. Regulations change and move some of the physician's work to nurse practitioners or pharmacists.

You may have heard a lot of talk about the so-called STEM

shortage. STEM refers to occupations based on Science, Technology, Engineering, and Mathematics. Students are often urged to enter these fields, and jobs are presumably available. But are they really? Is biology in as much demand as botany? Are computer scientists in as much demand as pure math graduates? In fact, STEM is too blunt to be of any particular value.

Any particular skill set is subject to becoming obsolete with little notice. And any career coach who does not account for the forces of both competition and technology is providing advice for the moment, not for a lifetime.

Let's say you don't buy my argument that careers of tomorrow are anyone's guess. So you go directly to the best source of American job data: The U.S. Bureau of Labor Statistics (BLS). As it happens, the BLS does try to predict the future. As of January 8, 2014, it estimated which occupations would grow fastest over the period 2012 to 2022. The top 20 occupations are a remarkable collection of jobs, with widely varying skill levels. They include industrial psychologists (#1), insulation workers (#4), occupational therapy *assistants* (#8), electrician's *helper* (#15), and medical secretaries (#19).*

Those are the fastest-growing, but what about the occupations that will add the greatest number of absolute jobs during the same time period? The list includes registered nurses (#2); retail salespersons (#3); food preparation and serving workers, including fast food (#5); customer service representatives (#8); janitors and cleaners (#9); and construction laborers (#10). This list is not exactly a triumph of skilled work. Most offer relatively low pay. Again, this is because "good" jobs are disappearing, and this list is what's left. Moreover, while the BLS uses a credible model for making these predictions, it explicitly doesn't include any forecast

---

* http://www.bls.gov/ooh/fastest-growing.htm

of disruptive technological change.[*] Living in our times, it's hard to imagine there won't be some level of disruptive change.

All of this means that I have to tell the young that they live in a tumultuously dynamic world, where old answers no longer make sense and easy answers are hard to find. I need to remind them that when we look at the history of occupations, we used to see constant change. Now we see *accelerating* change. So do we ignore our history or try to deny it? This much is clear for sure: if we tell the young to pick a skill for a great career, we must be prepared to answer when they ask "which skill?" And, as I hope you see now, we simply cannot.

Argument #3: You're wasting time looking for a passion when you should just be doing *something!*

Don't succumb to paralysis by analysis, say the many people who argue with my point of view. Action is required, not thought. *Just start with what you can actually do and at least acquire some entry-level skills.* Then, the argument goes, work hard, with discipline and focus, and build mastery. As you do, you will become more valuable as an employee, and that value will offer rewards. As a bonus, you might actually come to enjoy the work involved.

This all sounds plausible . . . until you actually think about it.

So let's be rebels and think about it. First, where are you going to find this low-hanging fruit that will start your campaign for mastery? A subject you're good at in school? That's what many — maybe most — of my students have done. But already we have a problem.

High school subjects, quite properly, provide some founda-

---

* http://www.bls.gov/ooh/most-new-jobs.htm

tional skills that apply to many occupations. So to be good at a high school subject, or several of them, leaves a very wide range of choices. So where to start? The subject with the highest grades? That means you believe high school marks are much more accurate than even the teachers believe. And what about all the skills never addressed in high school? This same argument, by the way, applies to both colleges and universities.

Maybe you start your campaign by taking whatever job you can talk someone into giving you, or the highest-paying job you can get. This means your starting point in your skill strategy is near random, which makes no sense for such an important decision. You may be starting somewhere half-plausible, but where is the assurance that you've started at the place that leads to success fastest or most reliably? There isn't any, and I can hear the little ball bouncing on the roulette wheel of your life. As much as pro-skill people criticize the passion philosophy as irresponsible, I can't help but think that this random spinning of the wheel is much more reckless.

This argument always makes me think of Jack. He is the first-generation son of immigrants, and he knew his passion was product development. He wanted to have a hand in creating something, an opportunity to use his inventiveness. But when he graduated, he was seduced — as were his parents — by a job (not as a developer) with high status and immediate income. Five years later, he called me and said he felt trapped. We discussed how to find a job that allowed him to be an innovator. He was understandably anxious about making a shift. He had recently become a father, which was part of what made him anxious. And he had years of his parents' guidance in his head. But his newborn son helped make the decision for him. I asked, "What will you say to your son when he faces a critical decision? Will you be able to say, do as I say? Or do what I did?"

Seeing it from this point of view, Jack knew he would not recommend the roulette wheel approach. And so he resolved to move his own fate elsewhere.

Argument #4: If you develop great skill, then your passion will follow.

One of the most common arguments in favor of pursuing a skill first is that passion will come from mastering that skill. Sure, some people might actually come to have passion for their work, even though they chose it looking simply to build skill. But that's not assured, and those who find their passion this way do so accidentally. Luck has entered the fray, and as you will learn, I am not a fan of relying on luck. In short, I wholly disagree with the "find your skill and the passion will follow" approach.

Susan was a seriously high-achieving high school student. She was active in the school community and was a team athlete; she had a good mind and admirable discipline; and she excelled at all her school subjects. She could have entered many different programs of further study, but she chose accounting only because it was the most difficult to get into. (I see this all the time, by the way, and it makes me crazy. Really strong students choose the most competitive programs to apply to, not because they care about the subject but because they naively assume that, if the admission standards are the highest, the job opportunities must be the best.) Unsurprisingly, she was admitted. At university, Susan was still the good and diligent student who maintained a high class standing. But when she came to see me, she was concerned. Each year, she told me, it was harder to maintain her focus.

"Why?" I asked.

"I just don't care about the subject," she replied.

What should I have told this good student? "Just double down and one magical day you will achieve the joy of mastery! And then . . . then, you'll care!" No, I couldn't say such a thing. That would be like saying her feelings don't matter, and that she must soldier on. But if she doesn't care about financial analysis, why would the mastery of it give her satisfaction?

I will concede that mastery is a good feeling, and most of us enjoy having a sense of accomplishment, any kind of accomplishment: a game of golf well played and our golf buddies in awe; a meal superbly prepared; a set of financial statements presented without a single loophole. All such endeavors can be rewarded with that sense of mastery. Since I am severely challenged by the simplest household repair task, I am energized when I manage to reattach a stray piece of wall molding.

But do we really want to compare this general "I am not a total screw-up" feeling with the profound satisfaction of a valuable achievement? When we accomplish work that we care about, something that is important to us and to others, this feeling outstrips the power of random mastery. (It must be important to others or it is hardly a job for which you earn reward.) If you don't see how the pleasure of incidental mastery and the satisfaction of work accomplished differ, then you haven't experienced the latter for yourself.

The Counterargument: Your Trusty Prof Goes on the Offensive

Now that I've hopefully trashed these most common arguments, let's take a look at why I think passion *protects* — why passion is that extra layer of clothing on the temperamental spring day.

Let's return to Susan, the accounting student, for a moment. When she said, "I just don't care about the subject," what did I tell her? I said she must try to maximize her talent, and to do that, I challenged her to find the domain she cared about. I told her to try to be the *best* she could be, to find a career domain and to make sure her impact was as significant and wide-reaching as possible. Given her academic ability, it was easy to believe it could be very great indeed. I most certainly did not tell her to settle for less than what was within her grasp.

Notice that I did not tell Susan to strive for a particular job or specific result. Susan ultimately determined that she was fascinated by policy, and decided to pursue a career in the Canadian government, where she did feel she had the opportunity to stretch and use her talents to their greatest effect. But I could never have pointed her in that specific direction. You see, it is the curse of the economist to see everything in opportunity cost terms. It's never a matter of whether a decision produces positive or negative results. Questions such as *Did the investment work out? Did the strategy work out? Did the job work out? Was the product saleable?* are inherently flawed. The only question that counts is, *Have you achieved the best result?* not just a good or acceptable result. Did the investment earn the highest reward open to you? If not, you failed.

If you're wondering what this perspective has to do with a skill-first approach, the answer is, *everything.*

Don't misunderstand, skill does matter. It has a place. But it is not the starting place for the best use of talent. Passion is, and passion makes the highest skills possible.

Becoming Exceptional

I am not such a renegade as to dispute the assertion that more skill is better than less. It is. So, how do you build skill? There are two ways: education (including training) and practice (also called *ex-*

perience). Both take effort, discipline, and persistence. The question is whether that's enough.

For an intermediate level of skill, sure. But as competitive pressure rises, the standard of performance also rises . . . and will keep rising. As a result, every day a divide grows among the skilled: There are those who clearly possess *some* skill and can get *some* work done. And then there are the standouts, those who produce exceptional results. A competitive marketplace wants the standouts. These are the stars. Again and again, I have seen this distinction between the merely skilled and the exceptional.

It's hard to pin down what the exceptional look like, because while the "ordinary" come in vanilla, the stars come in many flavors. To begin with, the exceptional tend to have *broader domain knowledge*. They know more about their subject across a wider range of topics. They have read more extensively, and they have more opinions about their field. I saw this in my student Samuel, who asked a question in every class. His questions were always penetrating, and each one focused on a different aspect of the content. He always had some background information that he was trying to process. There was Melissa, who always asked a provocative question, one that was often a direct challenge to my original observation. She wasn't arrogant; she just had background information in her head that she was trying to integrate. Would you doubt that both of them had serious talent? That they were on their way to being exceptionally skilled?

Another characteristic of the exceptional is their *mental flexibility,* their ability to roam effectively among differing subjects, and differing aspects of the same subject. They're also adept at putting it all in context, at seeing relationships and connections. For instance, after a reference in class to the ancient Roman Empire and modern economic policy, two students came to ask for further elaboration. They were in different programs, neither of which was economics, and one was a recent immigrant from China. Both were well read in ancient Roman history and they were united in this interest. After I provided more information, they began a discussion about ancient Rome, one in labored English. As I left the lecture hall, they were still in intense conversation. Across vastly different cultures and life experiences, they were nevertheless kindred spirits. What they had in common went far beyond their fascination with a society long dead. It was the exceptional talent they recognized in each other.

Parker was another such student. Once he came into my office to ask about a specific aspect of the labor market. By the time the conversation had ended, we had discussed — in a connected train of thought — robotics, computation mathematics, artificial intelligence, demographics, political philosophy, and international debt levels. Do I worry about his employability, about whether he's entering a high-demand field? No, I do not.

Exceptional students are all *engrossed in anything new and creative*. They like new ideas and exhaust me with their comments about why things should be improved, how they could be improved, why they are not already improved, and their own visions of new innovations. Their minds seem to be stuck on fast forward, living more in the future than in the present.

If you think that most people are plainly not exceptional like Samuel, Melissa, or the students who were so interested in ancient Rome, think again. If you think that most people aren't capable of having more than commodity skills, think again. For there is one more underlying trait that all stars have in common. In literally thousands of conversations, every student who was exceptional had *a passionate interest* in the domain being discussed. I have not encountered a single student who had great skill who did not also have passion for the field of battle. Not one. And I say that after teaching 23,000 students.

Passion's link to innovative skill is clear. Passion brings an intensity of focus that effort, discipline, and persistence cannot match. Passion provides the drive that causes the mind to cross disciplines and topic boundaries. And I very much hope that my tablemate at that retirement dinner reads this, for it's passion that will move her son out of the basement and away from his fast-food shifts.

Hard Questions, Honest Answers

1. To what extent are impatience and outside pressures affecting your career choices?
2. What notions do you have about what constitutes a "safe" job?
3. Do you feel you are not and cannot be exceptional? Why?
4. For parents: Are you hoping for a "safe" career for your child? When was the last time you really examined your beliefs about what "safe" means?

THREE

How Logic and Evidence Will Find You Work You Love

I HAVE DIFFERENT VERSIONS of the same conversation with students all the time. I explain why skills aren't enough, and why passion is essential. Then we come to the point in the conversation where students say, "Okay, Professor, I get it. I need to be passionate about my work. I agree with you (or at least for the sake of the argument I do). But I have absolutely no idea what my passion is. How am I supposed to pursue my passion if I can't find it?" Keep in mind, by the way, it's not just the young who say this to me. It's the middle-aged and the old, the highly educated and those less so.

This is indeed a perfectly valid question. And I agree. If you don't know what your passion is, you really can't pursue it.

"Tell me what some of your interests are," I'll ask. Stereotypical as it is, many of the young men I work with will say "Sports."

"Great," I'll say. "Do you play on a team?"

"No."

"Do you serve as a coach or manager?"

"No."

"Bet on outcomes?"

"Occasionally."

It quickly becomes apparent to me that their "interest" is really just in watching their favorite players pursue *their* passion on television.

The answers I get from my female students are only marginally more coherent. Usually they tell me they like to help people, but they don't volunteer, or work with people, or do anything other than perhaps serve customers at restaurants.

If it seems like I'm merely reciting stereotypes and clichés, well, you're right. But I report what I see and hear, and this is indeed the way many people think about their destiny.

The answer to this most common of questions, "How do I pursue my passion if I don't know what it is?" is simple, if not always welcome: You need to *work* to find your passion.

"But I *have* been looking," the student insists when I suggest she could be more proactive.

"How?" I ask.

"I think about it," she says.

"Oh? And what does that involve?"

"You know," she says, "I *think*."

Now, I don't mean to make fun of this student, who at least is putting some energy into the matter. But her answer to finding her passion seems to be staring into space, waiting for a revelation. This may work for Sherlock Holmes, but probably not so much for the average person in the real world.

Or there's the gentleman who tells me that he reads in order to find his passion. So far, so good. "And what do you read?" I ask.

"Oh, everything."

Putting on my interrogator hat, I press further. "Yes, but what specifically?"

It turns out he reads a blog posting here, a social media comment there. Sometimes he even reads big, heavy books, and I congratulate him. But I still tell him he's going about it all wrong, that reading simply what happens to land in front of him is no more sensible than waiting for lightning to strike.

Again and again, these searchers are unable to describe how often they search, where they search, and their strategy for searching. At best, their searches are improvised, casual, and effectively just random. There is no sign of focus or persistence, nor any hint of creativity. I want to collect all these people together, look them in the eye, and say, "Do you really believe you will find your passion in a bar or on MSN's home page?"

It all boils down to this: Far too many people seem to believe in the advertising tagline of an ancient movie called *The Last Starfighter:* "He did not find his destiny. His destiny found him."

So let's get serious. You *are* looking for your destiny; you are looking for your life's work; you are looking for the arena in which you will do battle; you are looking for your personal pathway to accomplishment; you are looking for the realization of your talent; you are looking for the epitaph on your tombstone. That is what a great career is. Chapter 3 will guide you through how to find it, but if you don't think this will take some focused work, you are sorely mistaken. I'll promise you this, though: it will be worth it.

The Overwhelm

It feels overwhelming—even impossible—to figure it out. In all the conversations with my students, and in all the correspondence I have with people around the world, this is the sentiment most frequently expressed.

Let me start with some validation. Yes, it's overwhelming. Finding your passion is not a simple or straightforward process. It's a little like finding your life partner. Sure, some people stumble into their mate by accident and never look back, living happily ever after. But these are the lucky ones. And yes, they do exist. Life, however, is not fair, and not everyone will be lucky. And so relying on pure luck is an invitation to disaster. Most people will have to fight to find their way. They'll have to earn it in a way the lucky will never fully appreciate. Indeed, for most, the path is filled with twists and turns. *It's hard*. But so what? Again, the important point is that it's worth it.

What's more, there are two very legitimate reasons why it's so overwhelming. The first is that, just as with choosing a partner, when choosing a passion to pursue, you need to listen to your emotions and also to be logical at the same time — but not too much of one or the other. The second reason is the sheer number of possibilities available.

Let's break the first reason down. On the one hand, the emotional side of you must care deeply about the work. You need to honor that part of yourself and not dismiss your love for, say, surfing, just because your rational brain is running through the improbability of ever finding a job riding waves at the beach. On the other hand, if there's too much emotion involved, you're in trouble because you're not thinking clearly. You can go through an entire range of emotions about work you think you love, like nursing, and get so captivated by the romance of it all — by the image of yourself as Florence Nightingale, for instance — that you walk right past your passion. The same emotional thinking is present — and dangerous — when it concerns a career that you're certain you *don't* want.

The Emotional Seeker will say things like, "Oh, I could never be a realtor. That doesn't appeal to me at all. I could never do it."

"All right," I'll say in return. "Why is that? Do you know how a realtor spends most of his day? Do you know the skills needed to be a good realtor? What their backgrounds tend to be, and why?"

The Emotional Seeker does not know the answers to these questions. The Emotional Seeker has a vague sense of the realtor as someone who drives people around and looks at houses. He hasn't stopped to consider the negotiating savvy, the people skills, the understanding of a complex market, and the creativity to grasp the potential in a house that just needs some cosmetic help.

"But Professor," the Emotional Seeker says, "you're always telling us to be passionate. If I don't feel that spark when I think about being a realtor, shouldn't I listen to that feeling?"

Here is where I roll my eyes. This is not Romeo and Juliet, where eyes meet and the world stops. Passion is not instant fireworks. And when the Emotional Seeker is talking to me about a spark, I can't help but think he's using emotion as an excuse not to do the work of gathering the necessary information. So let me say it plainly: Get the facts! Know what you're pursuing, and then if you still don't think it's for you, fine. But at least you're working with all the available data.

Just as Emotional Seekers are liable to walk right past their passion, they're also vulnerable to being so committed to their passion that they ignore all the warning signs that it's a bad fit. Who doesn't know someone who's in a dysfunctional relationship, but willfully, stubbornly refuses to see it? "But I *love* him," your friend might wail, as you list all the ways her partner has betrayed her.

At the other extreme, we have the ruthlessly rational Logical Seeker. The Logical Seeker will get so caught up in amassing facts and observations that she forgets the goal is to become energized by her mission.

"Look at this spreadsheet!" she might say, with something akin to passion. "Clearly, given my qualifications and the areas in which

I've excelled so far, the marketability of this subset of skills, the promotion rates, and the rates of return to educational designations, I should be a software engineer."

"But do you *love* it?" I ask. "Do you think you would do it even if you won the lottery and didn't have to work?"

The Logical Seeker is likely to engage in an argument with me about the improbability of winning the lottery, which of course isn't the point at all. The point is would she choose to be a software engineer even if she didn't need a salary?

What's the answer, then? Hard as it is, you must utilize both emotion *and* logic in balance. Use emotion to drive your search and logic to make your choice. Fact and emotion power each other; neither is subservient to the other.

I had two students who were passionately interested in political affairs and public policy. Both wanted to have impact on their world. One decided that he would seek political office as soon as possible. He created an overall plan that started with an immediate run for municipal government and ended at the highest office in the land. He focused all his research solely on the mechanics of winning elections. However, his plan was wildly unrealistic, given that it had a thirty-year time horizon and assumed conditions that were unknowable. It was all emotion and little logic.

The other student had an equally strong concern for public welfare and policy. But his reading of recent history led him to believe that political action was futile. "It's just uninformed politicians responding to apathetic and ignorant voters," he complained to me. He became very discouraged and sought refuge in cynical inaction. Both of these young people had let themselves yield to emotion, and each had arrived at a different but equivalently unhelpful conclusion.

Both needed a cold shower — of logic and evidence. The first had to understand that he was living in fantasy land; the cynic needed to understand that he was part of the problem.

I finally persuaded both of them to do their homework, to read widely and to look for *practical* ways to satisfy their political passion. The first student is now preparing to become a political strategist, working in the backroom where, arguably, most of the power is. The second is working on data analysis in order to increase voter turnout. Now they are both pursuing their passion and have the chance to make useful contributions sooner rather than later.

Now back to the second reason why finding your passion feels so overwhelming: the vast number of possibilities. I teach economics, and so I'm more captivated by numbers and probabilities than the average person. I'm a self-professed numbers junkie, actually. As such, I see the challenge of finding passion through a scientific lens. How many careers are there? There are hundreds or thousands, depending on how you define them. The total number of occupations is at a record high. For every occupation that has disappeared, like typewriter repairperson, many new ones have emerged, like web designer and computer animator. How many topics of knowledge exist in which you might have an interest? Tens of thousands. In fact, there are more than you could ever learn about.

Our minds instinctively pull away from such limitless vistas. So again, when people tell me they feel overwhelmed, I agree that they have a justifiable reason to feel that way. But then they must stop feeling sorry for themselves and become what I think of as a thoughtful tourist. Like the tourist exploring a new city, you have a world of ideas and careers to explore. Like the tourist, you must also recognize that you can't explore all that is on offer. Like the tourist, you must plan your approach. But most of all, you must take as much time as you need to reach your final career destination. Accept that your journey may be long.

Sure, limitless choices are overwhelming, but that's a good thing! Wouldn't you prefer too many choices to too few? When there is a brick wall keeping you out of the city of your dreams, yes, you're probably stuck. But if there is a lush, complex forest obstructing your path, all you really need is a good map and a solid strategy to navigate your way through.

Step One: Start Where You Are

"I do not know where to start," the young person said. "Start where you are. Where else would you start?" I inevitably reply. You can hardly start where you are not. "Where would I go?" "Where you are not." This dialogue, which would do credit to Yoda and Luke Skywalker, speaks to the casualness with which many conduct their so-called career explorations. So begin by making an inventory of what you presently know about careers and your interests. It might not be a single-spaced, two-page list at first, but even jotting down a few items is a start. Start with writing down how you spend your free time. What types of books do you gravitate toward? What sort of conversations with your friends do you most enjoy? What types of projects do you embark on by choice?

Most people can define a few interests, and many of those do go beyond sports and helping people. But they insist that their interests are unrelated to career. Gerald, for instance, loved crossword puzzles, but it took me a good half hour of questioning to get that out of him.

"Why didn't you mention that before?" I asked.

"Who cares? Isn't it irrelevant?" he replied. But since he obviously cared, it *was* relevant.

Gerald was committing a devastating mistake, one that would greatly limit his chance to find any true passion. He was in my office to talk about his career, and he was subconsciously eliminating any interest that seemingly was not, on its surface, career-oriented.

"Don't you see?" I asked. "Being a crossword fanatic is absolutely relevant to career."

Gerald looked puzzled. "Professor, are you suggesting I become a crossword puzzle–maker? Because I don't think there are a lot of openings for those." His sarcasm was barely suppressed.

So what did his interest in crossword puzzles suggest? In addition to writing puzzles, it suggested such careers as cryptographer. In the popular film *The Imitation Game,* based on the life of Alan Turing, Turing screened would-be cryptographers by assessing their facility with crossword puzzles. But Gerald could do much more — he could be a computer security specialist, archaeologist, criminal investigator, linguist, game designer, toy designer, criminal litigator, auditor, and so many others, many of which I listed for him.

"I never thought about it," he said.

While Gerald was interested in crosswords, Jodi was interested in writing. But, like so many other sheep, she took a look at her English major at the end of college and just assumed she would apply to law school. Fortunately (and here is where Jodi became lucky), when an advisor reviewed her essays for law school admission, the advisor said, "All of your essays are about how much you love to write. Shouldn't you perhaps look at a career in writing?"

Jodi listened, without dismissing writing as an irrelevant possibility. She considered not only where she was, but where she had been. She recalled how she had asked for a typewriter for her sixth birthday, so that she could write a novel. She had written a children's book the next year, and a chapter book for her fourth-grade teacher. She had filled journals and journals with ideas and words. By mining her past and examining her present, by taking stock of where she was and where she had been, the path before her became clear. She's not a novelist, but she does work in publishing, and she writes almost each and every day.

But what if she hadn't encountered that advisor? What if she hadn't taken stock? She would have likely become like Jeff, a thirty-year-old who went straight to law school after undergrad because he didn't know what else to do. He didn't enjoy law school, but he'd started, so he figured he might as well stick it out. Now he works as a lawyer and does not enjoy his job at all. But the income is good, and he's thirty and feels he's at a point in life where he can't go backward and make less. He feels stuck.

It's not that Jeff's is a tragic story. He's only thirty, after all! He has plenty of time. But he must assess where he is, he must mine his history, he must look for the threads that have connected his interests, and he must not just rely on what the herds are doing.

There's also a completely different way of taking stock. Jodi realized her thread was writing, Jeff hadn't stopped to look at his thread, and then there's David. David considered his thread a weakness. And, truth be told, he wasn't wrong. He was actually a poster boy for laziness. He worked just enough to get the right number of credits to graduate. He actively looked for a low-stress, low-workload workplace where the salary was adequate. This gave him the personal time to do whatever he wanted, not that he did much. He saw his primary contribution to the planet as being a good parent, and he was indeed a very good parent.

So what's the problem, you ask? Nothing at all, except that he wasn't happy. He was bored. In our discussions, it came as a revelation to him that his laziness could be harnessed to a great purpose. All he needed to do was find a critically important problem, and figure out how a lazy person would complete it. Being lazy, we discussed, was just another way, albeit a perverse one, to express a desire for efficiency. I challenged him to mobilize what some would see as a weakness into a force for positive change. Half a year later, he had taken two separate jobs at his company — bookkeeper and office manager — and turned them into one by eliminating redundant and unnecessary steps. There was a significant cost-saving, and his employer is happy. David is not bored. And oddly enough, he is working with commitment toward becoming an efficiency expert. As is often the case, passion is attached to a kind of work rather than a specific occupation. David used where he was and where he had been, to focus on where he might go.

Step Two: Stop

Once you've identified one or more existing interests or threads of your life, what do you do next? Stop, just in case you're going to do something dumb. Some people are so desperate to find their great passion that they leap into the trap of "trying out" a career in their newly found interest. If Gerald had left our conversation about crosswords to enroll in a cryptology program, I would have been nothing short of exasperated with him. Rather, the value in identifying the crossword interest is that it suggested a broad direction in which to continue his search. Given the number of possibilities, that's a very great value. But it was not a green light to jump off a cliff and become the next Alan Turing.

People repeatedly tell me they tried this, they tried that, they retried some other choices. They made sure they gave their new job or new school program time to "grow on them." This crazed version of gardening — tossing seeds everywhere in hopes one might sprout into a beautiful flower — does nothing more than chew up many years of your scarce lifetime. This is why there are too many in their late thirties or early forties with a dozen careers behind them, and still they search. Of course, their desperation has only deepened, and now they range into even more speculative choices as they seek their god-given right to a passion. They are identical to the losing gambler, who makes ever greater bets to restore his fortunes. All in all, these disorganized, random walkers give passion a bad name.

Take Bethany. Bethany was a change junkie; she liked variety and followed her impulses. One year she was committed to music and worked for a record label. The next year she was a Hollywood nanny. Then she moved to the corporate world, working in advertising, until the next great calling summoned her. One day she discovered to her horror that many of her friends were far ahead of her in terms of both career and life. *It's not supposed to be this way,* she thought. She was at least their equal, and the status quo looked unfair to her.

Bethany was stirred to take action, which, ironically, meant to stop. Instead of jumping from one thing to the next, she committed to staying in one place. It took a lot of effort on her part, as she learned that sustained effort was not boring. Instead of acting like that crazed gardener, she took the approach of thinking her options through and researching. It was most certainly not easy; she told me her head was aching and that she had to stop herself from trying yet another fresh approach. Fortunately, she persisted, with one relapse, and carried her work — this time as a concert impresario — through to a successful conclusion. And that is exactly what she needed: a reward for patience. Recommending patience is never as effective as enjoying the benefit of the harvest that comes at the end of a long growing season.

Does that sound too "academic"? Is it academic to know what you are doing? Is it academic to be informed about one of the most important decisions of your life? Then yes, this is academic. And free-spirited change-junkie Bethany is glad she took this approach, because now, with sustained effort, she has made serious progress in finding her passion.

For most people, stopping is as simple as, well, stopping. If you are frustrated that you are not making more progress with your interior design career, and you find yourself feeling drawn in by something like real estate, just stop. Have you done everything you can with interior design? Have you tried different paths for making that career successful? Have you talked to enough people and researched enough options within interior design? Think it through. And hang out for a while.

Step Three: The Great Sampling

And now, let me change from strategic guru to tactician. Because I don't believe it's fair to stand up on a pedestal and just say *Find your dreams! Follow the rainbow!,* get everyone enthusiastic, and then take my leave. No, I want to leave you with some real tools for going forward. Economists, it just so happens, have a remarkable set of tools at the ready. Instead of following random impulses, economists take samples across a wide field. As any mathematician knows, sampling is the only way to get command of a vast domain of possibilities.

You recognize, morbid though it is, that you will die before you could possibly learn about all the topics in which you might be interested. So you either: a) roll the dice, b) give up, or c) go the way of the economist and conduct an organized sample. It's up to you, of course, but I'd recommend option c. Here's how to begin.

Starting with your existing interests, you move outward in a spiral-like fashion to probe for more interests. How? It's terribly complicated, so get your notebook ready:

You read, you talk, and you think analytically.

Did you get all that?

Read

Read, but don't just read whatever happens to come across your path like the young man I mentioned a few pages earlier. Use the pathway I mention above as your guide, and read many different subjects from many different sources. Read trade books, textbooks, fiction, nonfiction, articles, magazines, blogs, posters, museum and gallery displays, newspapers, news aggregators, conference papers, advertorials, and so on.

Let's say, for instance, that the interest you've identified — and that you think might just be a passion — is food. Read *Bon Appétit,* subscribe to food blogs, read Anthony Bourdain's memoirs, read *Like Water for Chocolate.* Done? Great. Now, push yourself out of the center of your spiral. Are you interested in the creativity that cooking offers? Read about molecular gastronomy. (Not sure what this is? Exactly. So read and find out how cooking is being made weirdly scientific.) Might you be interested in the business aspects of food? Read restaurant and food trade journals. Or perhaps you're interested in what food represents to us historically. Read books like *Salt: A World History* and *Lesser Beasts: A Snout-to-Tail History of the Humble Pig.* The goal of this reading is to notice whether you are getting more and more interested, or if you are starting to feel satiated. If your reaction is the latter, food is probably not your passion. Let me give you another example. Fred got caught up in a news article about the geology of a new mining discovery. He was fascinated by the fact that a massive mineral deposit was the result of a meteor strike eons ago. So what, you might ask, does this have to do with a career? A lot, as it turns out. Fred now runs a geologically oriented tourist attraction.

Now, here's where my advice might surprise you: If a subject seems interesting in the sense that you want to read more, do *not* do so. The present goal is to *sample,* not to read in depth. Each subject or topic you choose to read about should be farther away from the previous one. You find treasure by searching both far afield *and* nearby. Each item you read appears either more interesting than the others or less interesting. You are probing, exploring, gauging your degree of interest in the objective. So, while you might have found that reading about astronomy was getting more interesting, you then realized that astrophysics was even more interesting. Indeed, astronomy might have qualified as a passion, but you find out that your greater love is astrophysics. By reading broadly, by stopping yourself from reading more astronomy, you were not misled into thinking it is your destiny. By maximizing the range of your reading, you increase the probability that you will find more interests, perhaps more passions, and, finally, you'll find that one of them will be your overriding passion.

Do not under any circumstances mimic the actions of a search engine, which says, *If you're interested in this, then you might be interested in this, too!* As everyone knows, someone who searches for a toy online will then receive ads for every child-related product out there. These engines essentially freeze your interests and make it easier to sell to you, until you are so bored that you shut off your computer and go for a walk. In the Great Sampling, you are trying to *find* something, not *sell* yourself something. If you stick to familiar ground, reading and exploring only connected areas, you are really selling yourself the illusion of thoughtful action.

Again and again I have been told how a book, a news feature, or a single article in a magazine changed the trajectory of someone's life. One person I spoke with read a story written by a pilot about the pleasure of flight. To his credit, he kept reading and exploring different avenues, but always his mind returned to the joy of flying. Now he knew; he had a basis for comparison. Flying appealed to him more than the many other endeavors he had considered. So he could and did proceed to become a pilot with confidence.

Someone else I know was scanning the business press and happened to see an article on bankruptcy proceedings. It struck him as interesting and, with more reading and conversation, fascinating. Who could possibly find it interesting to pick over the bones of a dead business, you might ask? He did. He learned how salvaging assets could save some jobs and lives. He learned how bankruptcy gave an entrepreneur a second chance and simultaneously served as a vital link in the flow of credit. That's what motivated him.

Do you think he was lucky he found that article? Perhaps. Or perhaps the fact that he read widely and voraciously for almost two years is the actual reason. He had started by reading about general business issues, finding that business topics in general interested him. But that was a very broad field, so he read about business processes, accounting as a business management tool, and the regulations affecting business. The last of these led him to bankruptcy. He had found his home.

Talk

Similarly, you want to talk to people with widely ranging interests, experiences, and backgrounds. I speak from strong experience here — the only reason I presume to be able to offer guidance is because my students have taught me more than I have ever taught them. They've taught me about the amazingly diverse accomplishments of humanity; they've taught me what works and what doesn't. No matter if you're usually the teacher — always be a student and it's amazing what you'll learn.

If you do not happen to have a ready supply of undergraduates cycling through your office as I do, you might wonder how to find these individuals in the first place. Not a problem. Simply look. Look at your school, workplace, community center, country fair, exhibition, public meeting, or any community of interest, virtual or real. Is it easy to approach near strangers? No, sometimes people are jerks, but so what? Just look further and with renewed determination. And I would bet serious money that most people will be flattered that someone's taken an interest in their career stories. People love to talk about themselves.

As with reading, don't *only* look close to home, but don't neglect looking close to home, either. Talk to your family and friends. They are, at the very least, accessible to you.

"I do talk to my family and friends," I hear quite frequently. "But they don't know any more than I do."

"Their experience is outdated," the student will say. "I want to look at my future here, not someone else's past."

Apologies from a humble Canadian, but those excuses are absurd. If your family and friends are older than you, or if they have different experience than you, then they know more than you about that. Next excuse, please.

This entire book is based directly on the past experiences of a very large number of people, some from many years ago. And that is exactly the point: the same strategy for identifying your passion has worked for a long time, and it is likely to work for a long time to come. Again and again, I have been told how a single conversation opened a floodgate of career possibilities. Again and again, I have been told how a single conversation changed someone's life.

Perhaps the problem arises not from the failure to talk with family or friends, but from how those conversations go. A productive conversation does not involve you complaining about the frustrations of your search, the luck of other people, or just general whining. And a productive conversation does not involve asking vague questions like, *What do you think I should do?* Instead, ask about the other person, ask about her interests, and ask how she discovered her passion. It works, I promise.

A young man named Ben was sorely deflated in his search for passion, and then he met someone who loved his work intensely. In Ben's short life, that was a first; he'd never encountered anyone in love with their job. Everyone else Ben knew — his family and his friends — saw a job only as a way to make money. It was what you did if you did not win a lottery. But if you had to work, the ultimate goal was to secure a job that paid a lot so you could retire as soon as possible. So it was for Ben's parents, and so it had been for his grandparents.

But one day Ben met a friend of his father's, a cabinetmaker. Ben made the mistake of asking whether the work was hard. The cabinetmaker clearly thought it was a poor question and delivered an almost-rant about the glories of cabinetry. He stroked the finish of a nearby table and made Ben do likewise. It was not, he thundered, about hard work, but whether your work fed the soul. Ben was taken aback. He had never even considered looking for his passion, but talking to the cabinetmaker made him change his mind. Ben actually wasn't himself interested in cabinetry, but he wanted the same gleam in his eye that this gentleman had. Ben set to work finding his passion; he wanted to imagine that he could one day himself berate someone for asking *is that work hard?*

Or there was Tammie, who met a funeral director who showed her how a dignified exit from life was both reaffirming and an important release point for grief. She was in nursing school and couldn't stop replaying their conversation. She wasn't interested in being a funeral director, but then again, she'd never understood the promise or depth of the job before. It made her expand her approach to nursing, and she gravitated toward hospice/end of life care, where she saw the impact she could have on a family's impending loss and perhaps help make it more meaningful.

If you are horribly shy, if the thought of talking to strangers terrifies you, the first thing I'm compelled to tell you is that you must overcome your shyness if you are to succeed. The second thing is that, in the absence of people to talk to, you must read about how other people have found their way. You don't have to have political aspirations to find value in David McCullough's biography *Truman,* for instance, or be religious to gain insight from the memoirs of Mother Teresa. Read about how *other* people found their way forward. Profit from the examples of others who changed the world.

Think Analytically

You cannot just read or talk. You must also have your mind in high gear. You must be fully engaged, reading and thinking to a purpose. You must be constantly saying to yourself about whatever book, fact, argument, or person is at hand: *Why? Why did they do this? Why did they not do that? What if they had done this? What if they had done something entirely different? Why don't they do something differently now?* If answers start coming quickly, your passion may be lurking nearby. But you must get those questions in the front of your mind. Yes, it is intense. Few people are practiced in the art of critical thinking, regardless of their educational background.

But you will never find your passion simply by surfing or browsing the Internet. Recognize the superficiality implied by those words — *surfing* and *browsing* — and by our impatient, thoughtless world. You will have to stand against the tide of popular culture to find your passion, and that is not a simple task.

Alex, for instance, was the privileged heir of a rich family whose wealth had been created over several generations in the resource extraction business. His family knew they would have to make big changes in the future. They hoped the next generation would lead the charge into the twenty-first century. But Alex's family was smart enough to let him find his own way forward, supporting his career goals as long as he was thoughtful and applied his talent. Still, they did hint that they would like him to apply himself to the family business. The problem for Alex was that the weight of the wealth he would command was intimidating. He wanted to use it effectively but felt torn between his family's interests and his own. In a perverse way, his supportive family made it worse; if they had pushed him in one direction, he would have pushed back and done the opposite. Now he had to decide for himself. In this case, as in so many others, our discussion involved the many alternatives and how to rank them. It was in fact a discussion about strategic mastery. When he saw it that way, and saw himself as an orchestrator, his first steps were decisive. He would join the family business, but he was clear that he wanted to work for someone else first, to learn skills that would be complementary to what he would be doing with the family business, and to gain experience from the employees' point of view. He set goals and timelines and informed his family of his intentions. The bottom line is, thinking analytically works . . . even for the rich.

The Great Sampling is the MVP of my toolbox. But many people will want more tools. They will want tests, courses, checklists, or other techniques that will help them identify their interests. Plenty of these tools exist. Some are clearly credible, with research to back them up. Others are not.

Many of these tools can be very helpful, but they should be taken as merely a step in the research, not as a shortcut. Do not — I repeat — *do not* take results that gently point you toward a career in finance and then immediately enroll in an accounting course. This is the equivalent of taking diet pills. It might make you feel like you've got a handle on it, but it is not a lasting solution in the end. You have to do the hard work of reading, talking, and thinking analytically. You have to do the important work of the Great Sampling.

So look at additional tools as just that—aids to help you do the hard work. They can increase the number of starting points for your continued exploration. They can reduce the danger that you'll miss considering a potentially fruitful line of inquiry. So by all means, check a few out if you'd like—just make sure they're backed by research. And always remember that no tool can tell you what your interests are. A tool can only tell you what your interests *might* be. Finding your true passion is too important to trust to an automated calculation, and there is no substitute for your own hard work and research.

Step Four: Recognize Your Passion (vs. an Interest)

Imagine a man wants to propose to his girlfriend of several years. He takes her to a beautiful bluff overlooking the ocean. They have a picnic, drink some champagne, and then when she stands up to wipe some crumbs off her shirt, he gets down on one knee. "Darling," he says. "These past years with you have been fairly conflict-free. I think we are very compatible. I find you very interesting. I think we should spend our life together, if you will agree to marry me."

Oh, this poor man. If he is lucky enough not to be shoved off the bluff by his girlfriend, he will at the very least be dumped by her. That would probably be a smart move, for he clearly does not love her passionately. He is merely *interested* in her.

The rule of passion is simple: The mind cannot stop thinking about that which it loves. One moment you are reading in hopes of finding a topic of great interest; the next you find you are reading and do not want to stop. It almost feels that you *cannot* stop. Or you find yourself in a regular conversation, and you start talking with excitement about an idea or possibility. Or you find yourself in an activity and you lose track of time itself, you're in your "flow," or "genius zone," as various writers have called it.

For some, the realization is sudden. But it's not magic. It's based on reaching a critical mass of experience, so that realization bubbles up and coalesces into a complete and compelling vision. (Leave it to an economist to take all the magic out of a revelation, right?) For others, it is a slow process, each piece coming into view separately until the pattern is revealed.

If you're stuck wondering if your interest is a passion, you can think about the proposal story. That is, if your interest were a person, how would you propose? You can also look carefully at the problems surrounding your interest. Are you fascinated by them? For example, I'm interested in biology. The complexities and interactions of biological systems seem amazing to me. But I have zero interest in solving biological mysteries. It's not just that I do not know enough to do so, the truth is, I do not want to learn enough to do so. And that leads us to another indicator of passion: The Teacher's Rule.

Teachers know that the best students learn easily because they love the subject. "Easily" does not mean quickly; "easily" does not mean without frustration and errors. What it means is that these students are driven to find answers, to overcome whatever obstacle appears. They learn their subjects because they *have to*.

But if there is no passion for learning, there is no passion of any kind. So test yourself. Once you have found a candidate for your passion, find an introductory textbook and find out if you *want* to teach yourself something. (Yes, I suppose this is what you would expect a professor to suggest. But that doesn't make it less true.)

Step Five: Keep Looking

Now that you have identified a passion, don't start worrying about whether it is or could be a career. That question is premature. As soon as an interest qualifies or appears to qualify as a passion, put it aside and keep looking for *another* passion.

At this point, you probably think I'm being unreasonable. But just because you have found your love, it does not mean you have found your *greatest* love. For want of patience, you might walk past your destiny. So keep searching and tilt the odds even more in your favor. Just as the gentleman who was captivated by the pilot's article about flying came back to it, you will return to your true passion, as well. And you'll be all the more assured that it's the right career. Remember Jodi, the would-be lawyer who became a writer? After she identified her passion, she took some detours. When jobs in publishing were not available in abundance, she tried public health and experimented with social work. And still she came back to writing, even more convinced that, although the road to do what she loved might be challenging, it was what she loved most of all.

Too Many Passions

"Professor, I feel like I'd be just as happy being the next Einstein as the next Beethoven." The young man was clearly fretting.

"Excellent!" I replied. Having multiple passions is wonderful, not a disadvantage to be anxious about. Yet this young man is not alone in thinking it's a predicament. I would say that the only reason it's perceived as a problem is because we live in an unimaginative, linear world. We live in a world that asks you to check off a single box for what you do.

What if, instead of checking off a box, you got to write a full paragraph explaining your work? This isn't what the world asks you to do, but it's what you should do. Those who are fortunate enough to have many passions should try to combine as many of them as possible into an integrated career. For example, I've known engineers who work in the entertainment industry, using their engineering expertise in unusual ways. As I discussed in the introduction, I am another example; I teach, yes, but I'm also an economist — economics is another one of my loves. I'm passionate about technology, and I advise students about their technological ventures. I've forged my own path that allows me to integrate what I love the most into my work — and though it has taken effort and has required creativity, I've not done anything that anyone else could not do. If you can escape the limited constraints of conventionality — and the key there is not feeling you must tick off any one box — then you can combine several passions to create the career you want. (I will go much farther into this in chapter 12.)

Then there is the individual who has difficulty figuring out which of her passions should be the basis of her livelihood, and which should remain her personal pleasure. For instance, a middle-aged attorney spent each and every one of her weekends skiing in the winter. From the moment the weather turned cold in November, she checked ski reports obsessively for signs of fresh powder. Did this mean she shouldn't be an attorney? That she was truly meant to be on ski patrol instead?

Not at all. The question at hand here is whether she lived for the weekends or enjoyed her job. In this case, she loved her job, and skiing fit into her life perfectly. She was a multifaceted person, living a well-rounded life, and there's nothing I could recommend more.

How Much Time?

"I'm interested in anything — for a while," wrote Summer. "Even obsessive about things — for a while. And then I get bored. Maybe my personality type isn't career-passion capable. Maybe you are lecturing to the lifeless masses about what only a tiny proportion is actually capable of sustaining."

"My passion isn't very concrete," wrote Barbara. "I have often felt excitement when I start creating things or figuring things out in different areas . . . My ideas of what I'd do lie in these vague feelings of 'creating' and 'learning' . . . I thought if I tried hard enough to incorporate creativity and learning, I would fall in love with any job in my way, but I don't . . . Now I'm left searching for what I'm meant to do, and I have to overcome all these external and internal voices telling me to 'stop and settle.'"

I've heard concerns like these many times over, and others as well: How long should the search for interests continue? When do you stop — when you have enough passions to choose your greatest love? Do you stop searching if all you can find are interests and no real passions? When do you settle for a career based only on interest?

All these are valid questions. And I do have answers, but first it's important to recognize the mind's natural tendency to resolve painful uncertainty by rushing to judgment . . . even to the judgment that it's time to give up. Be aware of your own bias, and recognize how your brain might be working against you and your capacity for patience.

I do not believe that any personality type is incapable of finding a sustaining passion. The 23,000 students I've worked with over thirty years are proof that, contrary to Summer's suggestion that I'm lecturing to "lifeless masses," the majority of people — not a "tiny proportion" — are capable of finding their passion. Quite simply, I've seen it. My guess is that Summer is surrounded by people who seem worn down by their work. So it seems to her that you have to be remarkably exceptional, blessed by the gods, to enjoy your work. But I know that's not so.

I know because I have watched a small army of people find their passions. Some found it in esoteric fields, others in working with their hands; some in the most rigorous domains, others in highly artistic endeavors; some in solitary labors, and others in massive teams. They came from all backgrounds, immigrants and native-born, the affluent and those who could barely pay their rent. All personality types were represented. Some were shy and others loud; some were aggressively confident and others fearful. The only thing that united them was their passion. It is not exceptional for people to find their passions, it is not reserved for the select few. But I will say that the vast majority of them searched method-ically and with determination to reach their goals.

In one sense, yes, there is a limit to how long you should search and how extensive your Great Sampling should be. While it will al-ways be a judgment call, there are some benchmarks to guide you.

First, the decision is affected by your age. If you're young, you have the luxury of a longer search, perhaps of several years. If you're older, you need to stop sooner, but you should take at least a year. Does this mean you're devoting all your waking hours to this? Not at all. That's why a key determinant is not the length but the *intensity* of the search. If you attend school or have a job, you might spend a couple hours searching on most days. At that rate of intensity, a well-rounded search over a year should cover a lot of territory and have a high likelihood of success. Two years at that intensity is even better. (Just so you don't think I'm nothing but an out-of-touch taskmaster, clearly not everyone will be able to spend a couple of hours a day. For example, the parent of young children will likely move more slowly.) You'll know you've been successful in your Great Sampling if this time yields at least a couple of strong interests or passions.

The question of how long you should search, however, is mis-leading in and of itself. It is merely tactical rather than strategic.

If you're young, search as long as you can before the demands of life require you to take a job of some kind. But taking a job doesn't mean you stop searching. It just means you search intermittently.

Life pathways are highly varied. Any number of circumstances can set us off on roundabout journeys. Becoming ill or aiding an ill family member can deflect our time and attention. Finding the love of your life can be so overpowering that career fades out of view for a time. The incidental accidents of life can therefore displace the search for interests and career passion. It is understandable that someone might find himself married and "working for a living," without either an identified interest or passion. But that is no reason to give up finding one. In these circumstances, you cannot search aggressively or continuously. But you can search nevertheless, whenever you can, however you can.

Alec was a well-paid machinist who was seriously bored. Every night he complained to his spouse about the monotony of his job. Finally, she told him to either stop the whining or do something about his discontent. (Bless the spouse who knows when to be supportive and when to raise a ruckus.) So Alec took a night course in literature and surprised himself by doing well. Six years later, he's far from where he started — he teaches senior English at a private high school. And he couldn't be happier.

Flora was a high school dropout who went from one thankless job to another, a single parent who struggled to pay her bills by working as an administrative assistant. But she was a fighter, a quiet, steady woman who thought she deserved better. She experimented, read, and talked to friends and family about how they'd found their paths. Finally, there it was — a job worthy of her talent and interests, a near-perfect blend of her interests, personality, and aptitude. Finally, she is happy as a veterinary technician, working with animals she loves all day and using her experience and people skills to excel. A better role model for her child would be hard to find.

So how long do you search? In pursuit of your passion, you search as long as you have to. As long as you search, you have at least the hope that tomorrow your talent will find its true home.

What's more, once you've found it, and achieved it, be open to changing. You change, and the world changes. Priorities shift, new opportunities and crises can arise. While you must pursue your passion to realize your talent, there is an equal need to be ever vigilant. In other words, if you're doing it right, the search should never end.

Hard Questions, Honest Answers

1. Take an inventory of your interests over your lifetime. What patterns do you see?
2. To what extent is emotion driving your career choices? To what extent is logic? Is there a healthy balance of both?
3. If you won the lottery and didn't have to work, would you still want to do what it is that you do?

FOUR

The Most Common Career Mistakes

T HE FIRST RULE of investment is: don't lose money.

Similarly, the first rule of career is: stop making mistakes.

So we are going to look at the seven most common mistakes people make *after* they find their passion. Most of those who provide career advice try to strike an encouraging tone, and they are often reluctant to spend much time talking about what goes wrong. While I too want to offer an upbeat message, I want to show you *how* to have a great career, not just merely encourage you to do so.

That's why chapter 4 looks at mistakes cold-bloodedly; you need to see what *not* to do. Yes, there are a lot of proactive steps you must take for a great career, but first you have to get out of your own way.

Mistake #1: Has Your Passion Crossed Over to Dangerous Obsession?

To be sure, passion is about emotion, as it should be. Emotion, by its very definition, moves people to action. But emotion is all too often the enemy of thought.

Consider Jason, who is a passionate gamer. He discovered computer games as a young man and was mesmerized, as are many young people. But Jason had a true passion, he wasn't merely addicted to the games' rush. He was fascinated by every aspect of the computer game: its technology, story lines, history, creative aspects, and commercial potential. He then crafted a career plan to become an important part of this industry. He got an education that allowed him to secure a job as a technical developer at a credible company.

The problem was, the more he immersed himself, the more everything else was pushed out of his mind. Gaming became his entire world. His circle of friends shrank to those he played with who were equally enthralled. These passionate players talked themselves into a state of near obsession. Ask Jason about anything outside of gaming and you got a blank stare. If the subject of conversation was, say, movies, all he could talk about was which game would make a good movie. Naturally, he grew more isolated.

Then his career took a turn for the worse. Jason was already aware that his technical role had not grown to allow him creative input, or any kind of input at all. He just coded, as he was told to. If he made a suggestion to his higher-ups, it went nowhere — not surprisingly since they didn't want to engage in extended conversations with him. Even among other employees, he was known as being over the top in his zeal for gaming and nothing else. Who knew whether his ideas were any good or not? They were never tested. His discontent about that became irrelevant when he was finally let go. Sales were weak in the hypercompetitive games market, and Jason was downsized. He was one of the first to be terminated, since his value was simply coding — an easy role to replace if sales rose again.

Since Jason's passion was so strong and genuine, he was completely confused. Wasn't passion the key thing you needed to succeed in your career? Hadn't he done everything right? You might suppose he'd learned he *wasn't* doing everything right. But when we spoke, he could not break out of talking about how much he loved his work and the industry. Why couldn't everyone else just see how cool his ideas were?

I would like to say I helped him. I did not. Jason was not prepared to accept that he was making any kind of mistake. And so he believed he just had to keep trying. These days, Jason still labors in the lower echelons of gaming companies, moving from one entry-level position to another, hoping that the next job will be *the one*. But if I couldn't help Jason, maybe Jason's example can help you.

Jason let his passion rule his mind. He forgot to think, to create a plan, or to find his distinction. Passion is without a doubt a powerful motivator, but like a powerful dragon, much beloved of gamers, it needs to be reined in. Reined in, your passion can take flight into great adventures. Otherwise, your dragon might just incinerate you.

Mistake #2: Are You Using Passion Itself as an Excuse?

Martha's passion took her in a different direction. An intensely curious person, she was also, as she told me, a naturally passionate person. She cared a lot, and cared about a lot of things. Martha was also very smart, well read, and had had an excellent education. As a result, she could speak articulately about her many passions, telling you exactly why they were so important to her and to society. These arguments were almost always very persuasive. In addition, she had multiple skills that offered her a variety of employment opportunities. What could go wrong?

Unfortunately, like Jason, Martha had no sense of mental discipline. She started a job in a burst of passionate enthusiasm, and typically impressed her employer ... but only for a few months. Then her reading and interests suddenly found a new passion in a new direction that she began to think about almost constantly. She became so distracted that her daily work performance declined.

As that happened, she became dissatisfied with her current job and concluded that her original passion for it was not as strong as she had thought. But that was okay since she had a "better" passion, and off she went to get another job. And with her skills, she got it. But then the same thing happened as yet another passion replaced the second one. And again after that. Of course, her job history began to look questionable. Martha was confused. How could a person like her, with so many true passions, have a career that was circling the junkyard?

"Remember that a great career requires having impact," I told her. "And to have impact in any of your passions, you must persist in one of them at a time."

"Professor, are you asking me to turn my back on my passion?" she asked, and smiled a wide "gotcha!" smile. She thought she'd caught me in a contradiction.

No such luck for Martha. For while passion is essential for a great career, it is not sufficient.

My student Elliott made a similar mistake. Firm in his belief that he could rely solely on his passion to carry the day, he planned to follow his passion and pursue his dreams. That was the most important consideration: everything else was just a minor detail, and thus his passion became his protector. He loved green buildings and their design. He recruited a partner and decided to start constructing green buildings. He listened to analytic questioners like myself patiently, deflecting every practical issue with positively fantastical solutions. Apparently, the government would provide help with funding. Apparently, he'd be able to rush through the standard periods of safety testing.

Now, Elliott was a smart and knowledgeable person; he was not delusional. But he was totally in love with his idea and blind to any objections. When his scheme came to an end, he took it badly.

What Elliott and Martha learned the hard way is that passion is not a justification for disengaging your brain. If you're looking for a simple answer that's easy to implement ("Passion is all I need!"), you're not looking for an answer that actually works. But if you're looking for a true answer that is multifaceted and works, keep reading.

Mistake #3: Are You Neglecting Your Homework?

The most common mistake afflicting those who have a disciplined passion is their utter failure to do their homework. While they may have a defined passion they are committed to pursuing, many people, like Jason, Martha, and Elliot, still think of passion as a shield, as though it will protect them from bad decisions. So these foolhardy souls plunge ahead without a realistic plan.

Harry's passion had intensified and defined itself. He began with a broad interest in science, which narrowed to biology, and finally he honed in on molecular biology. To move forward, he needed a graduate degree, which he was eager to complete. It would allow him to do research in an important field that fascinated him. So far, so good.

We discussed the grad programs he was considering, and I strongly suggested he visit the various schools, wherever practical, to make sure he found the best choice for him. But he then got busy and didn't even find the time to go to the schools within a couple of hours' drive. I later suggested he check out the publication records of the researchers with whom he might work, all available online.

"I have," he said, "and all the researchers have publications in my field."

"Good. And are the publications relevant to your area, and interesting to you?"

"I didn't look in *that* much detail," he said. "They're all big schools — I'm sure there'll be something relevant for me."

"That seems like a pretty big risk, Harry," I said. For he didn't *know* there would be something relevant — he only *assumed* it.

He looked confused, and a bit put out. "I'm following my true passion, though," he said. "It'll work out." He left the conversation probably feeling as though I was being unsupportive, or argumentative for its own sake.

Unfortunately, poor Harry ended up with the supervisor from hell at the school he chose, conducting research in an area in which he had no specific interest. All he'd gained from grad school was a credible degree and research experience of no value to him as he sought employment. Indeed, the research was so unambitious that it didn't come close to reflecting his passion. Harry found himself at the bottom rung of a very tall ladder. To illustrate, one of his peers, an unimaginative workaholic whose parents had chosen his specialty for him, was already several rungs above Harry.

When I saw Harry again, he was prepared to listen. Fortunately, though his passion was bruised, it was otherwise intact (which is not always the case when a career goes off track). We discussed how to get his momentum back and tactics to allow him to pursue his goals effectively. But he had to start again.

Another student, Sandy, came to see me because she wanted to switch her undergraduate focus to the skilled trades. She loved working with her hands, and sitting at a desk in a professional workplace seemed too much like what she'd already done as a student — she knew it wasn't for her. Her choice was well reasoned and could lead to work that was both satisfying and, usually, well paid. Again, so far, so good.

Then she started acting like Harry.

"Which skilled trade are you thinking of?" I asked.

"Any of them," she said.

"That's a bit like attending university and saying you'll take any class," I countered. "Skilled trades are very different from one another. The training is different, as is the nature of the work and the working conditions themselves. The work of a bricklayer is quite different from that of an electrician."

"But they both work with their hands, don't they?" Sandy asked. "So I should enjoy either one."

Sandy's entire strategy was based on that single element, and while it was a good justification to move toward the trades, she had much homework still to do before taking action.

In the end, Sandy applied for all kinds of apprentice positions and trainee positions. She chose one merely because it seemed "best." In short, she didn't do her homework. Now, ironically, she's back staring at a computer screen, in the very type of job she'd most wanted to avoid.

Donald finishes out my trio of homework shirkers. Donald's passion was meteorology.

"What are the job conditions like for meteorologists?" I asked.

"I think they're pretty good," he said.

Sensing he hadn't researched properly, I pushed. "Where exactly do they work? How many work in a given place? How many job openings are there, usually?"

"Prof, why are you trying to discourage me?"

This was his first and really only reply. Passion had so colored his brain that asking a question about his career choice was considered discouraging. Do you see how dangerous this impulse was for Donald? His brain had gone on holiday.

"Donald, I'm not trying to discourage you at all," I said. "I just want this information so that we can discuss your next steps."

"Look, Professor, the job conditions don't really matter — I'm determined to do this, and I will, no matter what."

I cannot count how many times I have heard that line, career planning by clichéd determination!

Of course, the purpose of my questions was to find out how high the hurdles were, so he could plan how to overcome them. Instead, he was just going to run fast. And fall down hard, no doubt.

Again and again, I've seen scores of passionate people run after their dreams, their sight obscured by the fog of passion. They sprint ahead without knowing the most basic information about their goal, from pay scales to entry requirements to the number of potential employers.

The fault is not the passion. It is simply the lack of homework and the discipline to get that homework done.

Mistake #4: Do You Struggle to Communicate about Your Passion?

Toni wanted to enter advertising. She very carefully explained to me why she found it so engrossing. She had mapped out a very appropriate educational plan, one that showed a clear understanding of the job market after she graduated.

The problem was, Toni had poor communication skills. It took her a lot of words to make her point, she repeated herself frequently, and sometimes it was difficult to follow the thread of her argument. And I knew from our previous meetings that several of her summer job interviews had not gone well. I gently made this point and inquired whether she had considered her communication skills as a possible obstacle.

"Oh, yes," Toni said. "That's why I'm so glad I've finally found my passion."

I waited for her to continue. That's why she was glad, because . . . ?

But she had no more to say — that was the full extent of her reply. As we talked more, her thinking became clearer to me: since she'd found her passion, she believed people would find her words more compelling, more persuasive. I recognized this argument, since I once believed it myself.

When I was too young to know better, I had assumed that if you were speaking of a subject in which you were passionately interested, the words would naturally flow. You were, after all, speaking from the heart. But I learned when I started teaching that a lot could go wrong on the long way from the heart to the mouth. Yes, I loved both economics and teaching, but I was so nervous I mumbled. That and my shyness were badly slowing me down. Indeed, these deficiencies could have simply stopped me from achieving my goals. So I needed to fix these problems, or to give up.

I decided to fix them. I figured out what I was doing wrong. I redoubled my preparation. I reminded myself what I'd liked in teachers when I was a student. I stopped standing at the podium like I was a statue. With a lot of individual corrective steps and practice, I gradually got better. Unfortunately, I meet many people who are either unable or unwilling to put in similar effort. Perhaps they don't believe they can. Professors are notoriously guilty of leaving their communication problems unaddressed. Many of them truly love their subject areas, although their students would be surprised to hear so. They stand in front of the classroom, looking bored and disengaged. But they aren't — they just can't properly express their enthusiasm, and their students are poorer for it.

A professor might be able to get away with this failure, but Toni, headed for the advertising industry, would not. Her chosen career would require her to be very articulate about herself and about her ideas, in front of both her employer and their clients. Before she could succeed, Toni needed to learn how to communicate much more effectively. Indeed, among all those pursuing their passions, communication is essential.

If you doubt me, consider the story of Moe. Moe loved software development. He saw code as musical poetry, and he made it sing whatever song he wanted. The more complex the function he needed to deliver, the happier he was. At least, he was happy at the *start* of his career. He entered the job market with multiple offers with serious compensation.

Moe was so in love with software development that he bubbled over with new ideas. Indeed, being innovative is often a characteristic of the passionate and one of their most valuable characteristics. Remember, they cannot stop thinking about that which they love. But here is where the problems started. Unfortunately, Moe was limited in his ability to explain clearly, efficiently, and persuasively why his new idea should be implemented. It didn't matter whether his idea was narrow or broadly focused, since he couldn't make a compelling case either way. Naturally, Moe became progressively more frustrated.

"I wonder if I'd have been better off just being a code monkey," he said in my office one day, referring to the commodity coders who were, of course, utterly dispensable.

I knew he was feeling particularly frustrated that day, and that he was trying to be provocative, but still, the thought should have never been in his head. He had learned painfully that passion was not enough to get his ideas taken seriously. Moe admitted he "sort of knew" he had this communication problem.

"But I don't know . . ." he said. "It's hard to imagine taking time off from work I love, just to get training and to practice talking."

"Do you really care about software innovation?" I pushed. "Because if you do, you'll do what's necessary."

It wasn't his passion that was the issue — it was the discipline needed to work on his weaknesses in order to take his passion to a higher level. In this case, I'm pleased to report, Moe took my feedback to heart and put a concerted effort into building his communication skills. He has been promoted several times, and his frustration has abated mightily. He can now express the ideas that his heart and brain attach to so easily and express them with eloquence.

One of my all-time favorite stories on the subject of communication comes from my former student Ryan. Ryan truly wanted a great career, and he wanted everyone to take him seriously. So he took himself very seriously. Among other things, he never smiled. Curiously, he spoke easily, was helpful, and looked you in the eye. He was even friendly . . . sort of. But he never smiled.

He came to see me when he started to get adverse performance reviews. He was being rated as a poor team player. Ryan protested that this just wasn't true.

"I always try to contribute," he assured me, and I believed him because I knew him well.

When I noted that perhaps his demeanor was taken as disdain by his colleagues, he announced that this is simply how he was. Of course, if he'd come from a horrendous family situation, he might have an excuse for so somber a face. But he did not. So there was little choice but to tell him that doing a great job was just not enough, and that the obligation was on him to reach out to his team. No, he did not have to be the life of the party, but he had to build a better personal brand for the world he was living in.

Without a doubt he struggled with this issue, but he was determined to have a great career. His girlfriend coached him. And he learned how to smile — sort of. He worked especially hard on adopting a more engaging conversational style, making sure his team members understood that he liked working with them, because he did. Very occasionally, he even tried to be funny. Basically, he made sure he was not being misunderstood, and sure enough, promotions followed. See — these aren't all sad stories!

Mistake #5: Are You Simply Running with the Herd?

Billy wanted to be a lawyer, a goal that reflected his passion. He was attracted both to the intricate and historic structure of the law and its ability to guard the vulnerable. Added to this package, the adversarial nature of legal practice appealed to his competitive nature. So he happily headed off to law school. That's when we first met, and that's when, I'm afraid, I made him unhappy.

I asked about his plan, and it was exactly as one would expect. Get a legal education, serve the apprenticeship his jurisdiction required, pass his final bar exams, and apply for positions. He knew that the better his marks, the more likely that he would get an offer from a major firm. And he was prepared to consider practicing in a smaller firm, since it might offer a wider range of interesting legal problems. Billy fully understood the established pathway to a legal career and he seemed determined to achieve it. But I had to tell him how competitive legal practice was becoming, and that, in many places, an increasing number of graduates was saturating the market.

"What's your plan to deal with the competitive nature of your occupation?" I asked.

"I'll study more, so I get better marks than the others," he said.

"Oh, and what will your classmates be doing?"

He admitted that they would be doing the same thing.

"So," I continued, "are you intending to score better on your exams than they will?"

"Yes, I hope to."

Well, anything having to do with "hope"—luck's better-dressed brother—stresses me out, so I proceeded to stress Billy out. (Why should I be the only one stressed?)

I asked him to admit that he was relying on luck for the success of his career, on *hope* that he would graduate with classmates who just happened to be less committed, less intelligent, less focused, and less disciplined than he. "A heroic set of assumptions, is it not?"

Now he was really unhappy. "But what can I do?"

First, of course, he had to stop running with the herd. He'd received good advice about how to be a lawyer, but no one had really talked about the competitive legal job market. Billy had sensibly talked to several lawyers before applying for law school, he told me, and they were all encouraging. Of course they were—they were employed!

In fact, though, Billy did have a sense of how competitive the field was—I wasn't the first to break it to him. But he admitted, "I try not to let myself think about the competition because it's so depressing." And you might also be happier if I didn't remind you of this issue so often. But what's even more depressing than thinking about competition is being defeated by failing to think about it. By pursuing his career in the very same way everyone else was, by following the herd of other law students, Billy was putting himself at risk. He needed to look for an edge.

Since the law follows a prescribed route, Billy couldn't leave any of the normal steps out — he just had to add extra ingredients to make his plan more than a hope. For example, as soon as he began law school, he needed to figure out where he would serve his apprenticeship and start lobbying for a position. How? He could build personal relationships with lawyers in his chosen firms. How? He could get creative. Maybe he could concentrate on smaller firms and find a sole practitioner looking for a staged succession. There was a long list of possibilities. But Billy really hadn't given this any substantial thought.

In other words, Billy needed to sell himself aggressively from the beginning, when his classmates were merely studying in the law library. Fortunately, his competitive nature finally kicked in and a rather wicked grin came to his face. Billy came to the realization that there were battles to be fought *outside* the courtroom, and they could begin at once. Billy looked and felt much happier.

Anyone entering a competitive field — which is now almost all fields and will shortly be all fields — needs to stop just doing what all the other students and applicants are doing. And the same necessity applies for the ability to control your working conditions, including the time commitment, and for getting a promotion after you have the job.

My point is this: if your passion leads you to be in a competitive field, the sooner you start thinking of a way you can stand out or distinguish yourself from the rest of the competition, the better and happier and more successful you'll be. That doesn't necessarily mean just being at the top of your class. It's more about finding that perfect opportunity to apply your skills in a way that allows you to truly follow your passion.

Some discover this reality when they stop getting promotions. Indeed, it's this promotion issue that so baffled my former student Josie, who worked for a firm that engineered hardware. She did not realize the extent to which she was running in place. When she came in to talk with me, she was disappointed because she'd repeatedly failed to get a promotion.

"I don't get it," she explained. "I get all of my work done effectively, efficiently, and on time. I work well with everyone on my team. My performance reviews are good, and I work on whatever suggestions for improvement my manager gives me. But still, nothing. No movement."

"Do you do more than you're asked to do?" I asked.

"Yes!" she said. "But the problem is, so do my coworkers."

Logically, that would mean she needed to take her game up another notch. Clearly Josie was in a well-run organization where the standards for everyone were high. She would have to do more to stand out, not just more work, but better work. She needed to come up with a suggestion, a way to innovate to help her company.

Josie really didn't like that advice, and she recited a litany of reasons why. "Innovation wasn't in my job description. If it had been, I wouldn't have taken this job. I'm not creative — I've known that for ages."

I met her protests with silence, and so she continued talking. "Plus," she said, "my innovation might fail, you know, and then I'd be worse off. And it's not like the company trains us for innovation or anything, so they obviously don't value it. I mean, no one else is doing it."

No one else is doing it. Of all of Josie's questionable points, this one was key. She did not want to be doing anything her coworkers were not.

"Why are you so sure no one else is doing it?" I asked. "Maybe that's how some people are getting promoted."

"Doubtful," she scoffed.

"Okay, then why are they getting promoted, when you're not?"

She shrugged. "I have no idea."

"Josie," I said, "you work for a hardware engineering firm. Your firm repeatedly introduces new products — of course they're interested in innovation. They have to be."

"Yes," she said quickly, "but not in my division." She folded her arms.

Something was going on with Josie, clearly, and it became obvious to me that she was deeply uncomfortable doing anything different from others. She felt safest sticking close and, as a result, she would never stand out. She concluded that she would just have to work harder, without having any definition of what that meant. She was wedded to following what she saw as her workplace norms, and that was the end of it. If this were the *Leave It to Beaver* 1950s, Josie would have been fine. But it isn't, and she wouldn't be.

Remember, if you want to get ahead, you're going to have to do something or create something that allows you to stand out from the herd. That's how you will succeed. We cover this topic at length in chapter 6.

Mistake #6: Are You Allergic to a Plan?

I know the word *plan* isn't sexy; it doesn't call up exciting, liberating, or free-spirited images. I'll even admit that it might hint at boring, something you'd expect, say, a staid Canadian professor of economics to recommend. And indeed, I'm such a believer in a well-considered career plan that the entirety of Part II of this book is devoted to the subject.

But before we get there, you should know that I've been surprised at just how deeply negative the response can be to having a plan. For many, the thought of a plan is actually painful, if not scary.

I'm not sure how this word got such baggage attached to it. Perhaps it's because people so want to believe their destiny is up to fate and not within their control that they feel threatened by the very idea of taking the reins. Suppose you devise a plan to accomplish an important goal and it fails? The failure then falls squarely on you and belongs to you. On the other hand, if you did not plan, you can just be unlucky, and thus, a victim. Everyone sympathizes with a victim, right?

When I ask students and alumni about their career plans, I usually receive one of three responses: 1) "I have a plan!" (or so they say, when most of the time they do not); 2) "I don't need a plan" (but oh, how they do!); or 3) "I can't make a plan" (but, of course, they can). Let's take these responses in turn.

"I have a plan!"

Bob was one of the alleged planners, and, as it turns out, he was an urban planning student. So of course he had a plan — he wasn't at all afraid of the word. The plan was this: Step 1, get an appropriate education; Step 2, get a few good cooperative education internships; and Step 3, apply aggressively.

Did his plan have the flexibility to accommodate a change or evolution of his interests? Did it describe how he would distinguish himself from his classmates? Did it describe how he was going to choose and reach out to priority employers? Did it accommodate the possibility of grad school? What benchmarks was he using to decide if his plan was on track? How would he respond to graduating in a recession and finding no jobs available?

He had answers to none of these questions, and yet a good career plan addresses more issues than these. Well, actually, he did have one answer. "Professor," he said, "if any of those things happen, I'll deal with it then." Dealing with a circumstance when it happens is the opposite of planning. A plan tells you *in advance* what you will do in various scenarios and makes sure you are pre-pared.

I told him he was needlessly subjecting himself to risk. I told him that every time in past decades that the economy has weak-ened, I've been literally mobbed by students seeking guidance. Often the advice I give involves an action that they should have taken already. But because they waited too long, the best we can do sometimes is damage control — making sure that their career prog-ress is not even further slowed.

Let's play this out. During these downturns, many students sud-denly conclude, often correctly, that they should go to grad school. Now they need letters of reference, but none of their professors knows who they are because they haven't kept in touch. Deadlines for applications are days away; they scramble like crazy, some-times forcing a reference to write a generic letter instead of the more effective customized and personalized one. In their haste, they frequently pick a grad school that is not ideal and miss schol-arships for which they would have qualified.

Economic downturn aside, I also encounter students whose in-terests have changed over the course of their education. But be-cause they never imagined such a possibility, they are locked into a program of study from which they cannot extricate themselves without great cost. Of course, I try to help them make the change, but it is often far more costly in time and money than would oth-erwise have been the case. And sometimes the cost makes the stu-dents give up on their newfound dreams.

I explained all of this in detail to Bob the urban planner, and ended with, "Bob, do you want to take that risk?"

He concluded that he did not. With visible reluctance, he com-mitted to make a real plan. In truth, he looked like he was about to have a tooth extracted. But at least he was ready for it.

Betty was another supposed planner. She had done pretty well so far, in that she had worked in a career she enjoyed for a decade. The only problem she noted was that the workload was very high, and her personal life was suffering. I asked how she was planning to fix that.

"I'm taking courses and trying to work more efficiently," she replied.

"How will the courses help the workload issue?" I asked.

"Oh, well, the company encourages us to take more training," as she said this, she frowned, as if she could see she hadn't really thought it through. "I guess the link to easing my workload isn't totally clear."

I nodded. "If you work more efficiently, might the company not just give you more work?"

"Possibly," she admitted.

I continued with my badgering, which she took with good grace. I asked if her plan took the company's most strategic goals into account. Was her plan addressing the company's biggest immediate problem? Did her plan describe how she would craft and sell her personal brand? Again, there were no concrete answers. So in effect there was no plan, just some vague initiatives. That's better than doing nothing, but not by much. Betty reacted proactively to these questions, and she quickly began a real plan, one that saw her using her unique skill set and viewpoint to tackle the company's biggest challenges strategically, putting her in a position to better advocate for the hours and workload she wanted.

"I don't need a plan."

There are many people who say they do not *need* a plan. Why? Because their career is on track to success. With no problem, they assume there is no need to plan.

Of course, this just assumes that nothing bad will ever happen to you. Lurking behind this assertion, I suspect, is the superstition that, if you plan for a disaster, a disaster will indeed happen. Therefore, if you make a will, you'll be dead by the end of the week.

I am very sensitive to the wreckage that results from unexpected career mishaps because so many people seek me out when that happens. Sometimes I can persuade the complacent to develop a solid plan. Sometimes, I cannot.

Remember John, from chapter 1, who was classified as a 9-to-5er and summarily laid off? Originally, John was one of the bold ones who did not believe he needed a plan — everything was going great, after all. Then he suddenly found himself out of work. He had let his network erode, his finances were locked into high spending, including a big mortgage. His wife had an excellent job, and therefore his choices were limited by his desire to stay local. His skills were very focused and did not easily allow related work.

We cobbled together a plan for him, and through his own great effort, he secured another reasonable job, close to his passion. Oh, but did I mention that he commutes an hour and half each way every day? He's close again to doing what he loves, but farther from an ideal life.

The lesson here? Have a plan.

"I can't make a plan."

Those who fall into this category and say they cannot plan, even if they see the need to do so, are represented by Ella, a student I met exactly once. She is fundamentally a fatalist — what will be, will be!

While that might be a good song lyric, it is a terrible life choice. Yes, Ella can give you all sorts of reasons and clichés for her adamant refusal to plan: "Life is chaotic." "You never know what will happen next." "There are too many factors to think about." "The best you can do is to cope." While I undertake a good debate with relish, and I value the differences of opinion that spark them, the reality is that Ella and I have nothing to say to each other. When she finds herself out of work, she is likely to buy a lottery ticket instead of making an appointment to see me.

As you might imagine, I'm not a big fan of that approach to life, and I feel that people like Ella are making grave mistakes.

Mistake #7: Are You Losing Sight of Your Plan?

If you have developed a good career plan, you must still stick to it. Just like a diet plan or any kind of plan. Unfortunately, even those who create good plans still end up improvising their way into the future, because they often lack the discipline to persevere. They change their desires as quickly as they change their clothes. Or when the journey becomes hard, they retreat to what's easy.

If you're surprised to hear how often planning and discipline are coming up in this "inspirational" book about career, don't be. I want to do more than inspire you. I want to see you through to success.

I've told you some stories in this chapter that haven't had the happiest of endings, although all are still stories in progress. But if you've been paying attention and answering the questions in this chapter honestly for yourself, you can bypass these mistakes and go straight to the positive slant. Here are some "do's" to act as antidotes to the "don'ts":

- Keep your passion and your life well rounded.
- Be clear that while passion is necessary, it is not all that is necessary — do your research and your homework.
- Present yourself and your passion in a way that engages others.

- Always ask, "What is everyone else doing to get from A to B, and how can I do it differently?"
- Look upon planning as the sexiest thing in the world. Then have the discipline to stick to it.

Toward this end, the next chapters change course from mistakes and talk about what to do. And there is a lot to do.

Part I of this book has aimed to clear the clutter and to set the stage, so that the deeper work can be done. After all, walls need to be cleaned and primed before they can be painted. Illustrations need to be penciled before they can be inked. And, as I've just returned from helping my family make maple syrup, firewood must be stacked, equipment cleaned, and trees monitored before the sap can be collected. If you think making maple syrup sounds complicated, you're right. Imagine how much more complicated career success must be. So now that we've done all the necessary preparations, let's get our hands sticky and get to work. And that's what we'll be doing through the rest of the book.

Hard Questions, Honest Answers

1. When you considered the seven questions of this chapter, did you answer "yes" to any of them?
2. What is your plan for avoiding these mistakes? Or are you averse to planning?

PART II

CREATING YOUR CAREER PLAN

FIVE

Getting Yourself Ready

THINK ABOUT THIS for a moment: So much of our life is mapped out, on paper or onscreen. We determine the fastest route to the movie theater or shopping mall, taking into account the time of day, weather, and resulting traffic patterns. We plan out our vacations, booking hostels or hotels way in advance for the most popular destinations and the most popular times. You wouldn't show up in New Orleans for Mardi Gras without a reservation, and I can't imagine many people merely landed in Vancouver for the Winter Olympics without a place to stay and tickets to an event. As we get older, there is so much we plan carefully, from our weddings to home ownership to retirement. And yet, ironically, we don't put anything close to that much thought into planning our careers, which is one of the most crucial parts of our lives, and a major part from which so much else flows.

I ask — maybe beg — you to recognize how critical it is to develop a solid career plan, one that takes into account your personal hopes and dreams as well as the competitive economy, and one that leaves itself open to be adjusted as you go. A well-designed plan guards you from the dangers and mistakes I described in the last chapter. And a plan allows you to efficiently harvest the opportunities open to you.

Determine the Destination

I encounter people all the time who truly can't describe their goals precisely. "To be happy ... to be fulfilled ... to make a contribution ... to make a difference." None of those statements, genuine though they might be, is any more than a starting point for setting your goals. They're too general and vague in scope to support a plan, they provide no way to set priorities, to measure progress, or to evaluate tactics.

Heather understood this. She was on her way to becoming an accountant, and she was very happy about it. She saw accounting as a fascinating profession, where, with a relatively small set of numbers, she could predict the future and then shape the outcome of major corporate decisions. In other words, she and a balance sheet would change the world. With her passion clearly identified, she started to clarify her other goals. Since work was going to be such a big part of her life, she wanted her career and her life to be integrated right from the beginning. She wanted to be happy.

Her most immediate personal priority was to travel the world. Heather felt an absolute hunger to visit and explore as many countries, geographies, and cultures as possible. And she wanted an income that allowed her to travel in style. The life of a global backpacker did not appeal to her. She didn't want to sleep in airports or in bunkrooms with dozens of others, and she wanted to sample the local cuisine instead of subsisting on baguettes and cheese. Finally, "when the time was right," she was sure she would want a family.

So Heather's career destination involved the following:

1. Work in accounting that allowed her potentially to have a major impact
2. A high income
3. The opportunity to travel the world early in her career

Like Heather, Trent also started with the plan that he thought would make him happiest. He wanted to be a management consultant, and he had the education required for an entry-level job. Specifically, he wanted to help companies achieve game-changing productivity gains. He hated travel and wanted to live downtown in a big city. He wanted an active social and dating life. He did not want to work long hours. His primary financial need was enough income to afford a downtown condo. He also figured that among women he dated, one might qualify as a wife, eventually. As you can see, in his own way he was as ambitious as Heather. To put it in an organized form, his goals included:

1. A job in management consulting, focusing on productivity
2. A downtown lifestyle
3. A reasonable number of work hours without travel

Perhaps you think Trent and Heather are wildly unrealistic? Maybe, maybe not. But they are right to start with their fondest desires and then to try and get as close to them as possible. Think of it like real estate: No house-hunter goes into the shopping process without the starting point of a wish-list that includes everything they want. It's a powerful exercise.

On the flip side, notice how many people start with the totally modest goal of just an entry-level job related to their major. Then, if they achieve that, they think of what other goal they might add. Are you surprised that if you first dumb down your goals to almost nothing, you will struggle to get anywhere else? I know that in this competitively challenging world, you are often told by veterans of the system to be practical. By that they usually mean you should set your sights very low and pretty much forget about the dream of finding passion in your work. But remember that competition is the very reason you need to find a career you're passionate about. I want to be very practical about it all. I'm an economist, and we're the prophets of practicality. Planning your career is the passionate worker's answer to the need to be practical. And you must start with the best possible destination.

Ricardo had deep resistance to adopting goals for his career, never mind for his life. He was the child of immigrants, and so happy to be part of the first generation in a new country that he seemed all too willing to take any reasonable job open to him. And he did, as a manager at a bank. Fast forward a few years, and he was still there. No, he didn't love his job, but he figured he would try to have the best life he could anyway.

Ricardo had defined a passion, though: real estate. To him, a job in real estate would have been akin to winning the lottery, both in terms of the happiness it would bring and in the unlikeliness of it ever happening.

Is Ricardo more likely to succeed because of his more constrained choices? Is he wise not to tempt the fates by being too ambitious?

The plain truth is that Ricardo and his situation drove me to distraction. I hate waste of any kind, and that's what I saw with Ricardo. We live in a world where so much talent is wasted because people lower their sights from the start and think anything more is a bonus. It wouldn't have bothered me so much if Ricardo didn't have such deep talent. When he talked about real estate projects that had been built, he saw so many things wrong with them. But more than that, he saw so many opportunities to make them better, and countless missed opportunities to add to a project's profitability. And when he talked about what *might* be built, his visions were plainly impressive, sensitive to their environments, and often unlike anything he or I had seen.

Unfortunately, I could see him spending the next twenty years at his bank job, helping people get loans for homes or properties that were so much less interesting than what he might have created. And with his apparently unassertive approach to life, I could see Ricardo himself living in an average house with an average spouse and 1.5 average children, never seeking excellence in any of his endeavors. So what did I do in my frustration? I shouted at him to get *un*realistic!

It was indeed a struggle, but finally he got on a similar page to Heather and Trent. He allowed that he sort of wanted to be a developer. And yes, maybe he had fantasized about having a big family and living in the countryside. Now we had somewhere to begin. His destination was becoming clearer.

You too should set goals like Heather, Trent, and Ricardo have done. And then ask yourself if your goal, though it may be lofty, is also flexible. In other words, do you have your goal set at a pinpoint? You do not want that. If you are completely certain of exactly what company you want to work for, your goal is a pinpoint. If you are completely set on an obscure area of study or focus, such as weaponry of the third century, then your goal is a pinpoint. Broaden your range.

You may be thinking, *But you just told me to be precise*. And that is true, I did say that. But use common sense: a goal as broad as "I want to be happy" is meaningless, and one as narrow as "I want to do *this* job at *this* place" is only going to set you up for failure.

It's smart to have a destination, but in the uncertainty of the world, you need to give yourself wiggle room to accommodate changes. The market might change. *You* might change. Start with a broad range, and don't think about "narrowing" so much as you think about "researching." As you work at the task of researching, clarity will come on its own.

Distinguish Your Priorities

Having decided what would make them happy, Heather, Trent, and Ricardo needed to assign priorities to their main goals. This was the first step to practicality. Not everything might be possible at once. Again, it's like house-hunting. Perhaps you want a fireplace, but of the items on your wish list, where does it rank? Could you live without one if you needed to make such a choice? Could you add a fireplace later? Similarly, when it comes to career planning, each factor should have a useful measure of flexibility.

Heather identified factors that were less important to her and came to the conclusion that, of the great range of work she could do as an accountant, she could happily put her mind to most of it as long as she had a major impact on the outcome. So she had at least one constraint that was minimized. In addition, while she expected a relatively high income over the course of her career, a high starting salary was less important than the opportunity to travel. She'd backpack if she really had to.

Trent did the same thing and decided he was determined to work on productivity improvements and nothing else if he could possibly do so. He felt he was being flexible by not caring about exactly what *kinds* of productivity he would work on. He also concluded he might be willing to travel a little, and work longer hours than he wanted, at least in the beginning of his career. But condo life downtown was very important, second only to his work.

Do you think Heather and Trent are still too unrealistic? If so, do you not think they are better off finding out about what is feasible and what is not, rather than assuming it?

Ricardo and I continued our battle over the issue of priorities, because, although I'd talked him into telling me where he'd ultimately like to go, he assumed that none of it was really possible. It involved a lot of dialogue, wherein I asked questions like, "If you had to amend or delay part of your dream, which part would it be?" And Ricardo gave me passive answers like, "Any of it, Professor. Like I said, I can just work at the bank for the rest of my life, it's okay." And so it went on and on this way. We'll return to Ricardo in a bit, for a point finally came when we stopped going in circles and really made some progress on his plan.

So now you might try taking your own stab at this exercise, and do please use Heather and Trent as your models, not Ricardo. How do you rank your goals? Which could you make more flexible if you had to? What is nonnegotiable for you?

Identify the Specific Barriers to Achieving Your Goals

Now that you have begun to define your most desired goals, and to think about where they fall in terms of importance to you, the next step is to identify what barriers stand in the way. Aggressive goals, by their very nature, force you to think carefully about the obstacles. Obstacles you might have assumed were immoveable are not; you might not have noticed some true obstacles until they flattened you.

It didn't take Heather long to recognize the primary barriers to her goals. First, accounting jobs are usually rooted in one location—in one office, in one city. Second, in the beginning she wouldn't get anywhere near high-impact files. As a junior accountant, she would do less-interesting work, the boring stuff. And while her income would be reasonable, it was not "traveling-in-style" high. But it didn't matter anyway, because her vacation time in her early years would be modest at best. Over time, her vacation, income, and impact would improve, but by that stage she hoped to have kids, and traveling the world with babes in arms would only be harder.

Trent was also in an apparently impossible situation. With an entry-level position, he would have little choice in the work he would do, at least until he was older, like, say, forty (which to him was an eternity away). Moreover, management consulting normally involves long hours and a lot of travel. Or at least it would if Trent got a job with a major firm. The large firms typically had downtown offices, which was a plus, so Trent could live and work downtown and afford a small condo. But the problem was, he could only live there in between business trips. As a consequence, his social life would be transient, intermittent. By contrast, if Trent worked for a smaller firm, his income would probably be too low for his dreamed-of condo. Moreover, these firms rarely were located downtown.

So what should Heather and Trent do? Do both of them have to get realistic? Shouldn't Heather just pay her dues as an accountant? Get the best position available and travel on her vacations? Or if her travel bug cannot be delayed or denied, she could delay the start of her career and backpack the world, getting used to the appeal of youth hostels. And perhaps Trent needs to accept a long apprenticeship and choose which is more important to him: long hours and living downtown or less time commitment in a smaller firm in the suburbs. Surely, he could find a healthy social life in the 'burbs, if he had to.

Perhaps following the suggestions in the preceding paragraph is what "normal" people would do. But Heather and Trent were determined to have *great* careers, not just good ones. So Heather and Trent moved to the next step in their planning.

The critical point here is, there will be obstacles to the course you've set. List them objectively. Don't worry that you're being negative, don't think ahead about how to remedy them. At this stage, simply think it through and identify them.

Probe the Barriers and Revise Your Goals if Necessary

Heather and Trent recognized that there are always obstacles to accomplishment, and certainly to great careers. And barriers cannot be wished away, nor are intention and effort enough. The universe does not actually care if travel or downtown living is important to you, so wishing for a lucky break simply won't do. Heather and Trent decided that, if they wanted to have real workplace impact and to realize their personal goals, they would have to find a way to include them. Or strictly speaking, they at least should try.

Heather began her probe by looking for examples of how other accountants pursued unconventional career paths. Even if they weren't trying to travel the world, the unusual nature of their progress might help her see a way around her obstacles. The results, though, were not promising. Accounting—like many other professions, from architecture to engineering—has a relatively prescribed career path. Or at least it does if you want to stay in the profession and get your credentials or establish your reputation. The only accountants who traveled a lot were either associated with large multinational clients or were specialists who flew around the world to deal with exceptional situations. But those positions were restricted, not surprisingly, to highly experienced (that is to say, older) accountants. Heather, as I've said, did not want to wait. She had now clarified her career direction. And if she wanted to be an accountant, it was clear she would have to learn patience.

But there was another way. Heather could set aside the goal of being an accountant and pursue a career in quantitative analysis. Quantitative analysts still work with numbers, so she'd still have her ledger book, but she would not technically be called an accountant. In other words, the way around the barrier was to rethink the conventional description of the job itself.

Heather gave the matter much consideration. She decided she would complete the requirements for an accounting degree, since she was so close. But she decided not to take the additional steps (exams and so forth) required to achieve an official accounting qualification. Heather understood what many do not: that passions do not always exactly fit established occupations. Her career plan now had a revised career goal. She would solve high-impact problems using quantitative analysis outside of accounting; in other words, she could still put her mind to work on why a company's product or business was stagnating, but she wouldn't be the company's accountant — she'd have a different title. Since she would not have the credibility of her professional designation to help her, she might have to compromise on some of her personal goals. But travel was still a high priority as she considered her next steps. (Let me be clear. The point of this example is not that accounting is a poor career choice. It is not, but it was for Heather. An occupation, a career, is great only if it is *your* passion and if it meets your other high-priority goals.)

Trent was struggling as he probed his obstacles. Large firms all expected him to travel, and the smaller firms he looked at offered pay that simply did not support his cherished downtown lifestyle. And few firms would allow him much of a choice in the type of job he worked on — he could not request to focus on productivity. He decided to check out every possible firm to see if there were any exceptions to the traditional approach. There were a few firms that specialized in productivity, but they only hired consultants who were much more experienced than Trent. As is true for many types of occupations and careers, Trent was too young and inexperienced to be taken seriously. (The same problem affects the older worker like Ricardo, who wants to change careers but lacks experience in a different domain.) So Trent needed more education to have any control over the nature of the problems he would get to tackle. And downtown living would probably have to wait. In short, Trent was on his way back to school.

Ricardo, meanwhile, had finally become convinced to seek what it was that he most wanted. With a decade of excellent performance reviews at the bank under his belt, he had the credibility to look for a junior position in the real estate industry. He was probably most qualified to be a salesperson, but what he really wanted was a project management job with a developer. Unfortunately, he had no experience at all in real estate, though he had done a decade's worth of reading on the subject. The road to being a developer looked long indeed.

I asked him if he might raise enough money to do a small project on his own — something modest, like a renovation of a store in a strip mall. It didn't have to be all-consuming; it could be a part-time endeavor while he continued working at the bank. "After all," I said, "the best way to start a career is to start."

"I don't have money even for a modest project," Ricardo protested. "No one in my family does, either. And a bank's not going to lend me money, given my inexperience — that I know for sure."

Ricardo could find more reasons not to do something than almost anyone I knew. You see why he frustrated me so?

"You don't have any relatives with a few dollars?" I pushed.

"No!" he said, but then was quiet. "Well, yes. I have an uncle who's well-off, but I'm not going to ask him for money. He's a self-made man — he'd expect me to be, too."

"Why would you ask for a gift?" I asked. "Why wouldn't you of-fer him an opportunity to invest in a project you've identified and designed?"

At last, Ricardo looked like a thousand light bulbs had gone off in his head. He had never thought of his extended family as *inves-tors.* Yes, he was too old to ask for presents, but he could offer them a competitive rate of return. Maybe he could even best what his uncle was being offered elsewhere. Ricardo immediately set about identifying a project to take on, and when he had one, he set up a business meeting with his uncle.

"My first business meeting!" he said when he called to tell me about it. The pride in his voice was clear. In Ricardo's case, unlike those of Heather and Trent, his obstacle had faded upon examina-tion.

The point of this phase is to *probe,* to determine what is rock solid and what is not. Are you looking for work-arounds? Are you making assumptions about defined job titles or careers that can be dismantled? Are you falling victim to conventional thinking? Are you rushing to *no* too quickly?

Identify, Acquire, and Strengthen the Key Skills You Need

When I argued in chapter 2 that you couldn't build a great ca-reer on skills without passion, I didn't say skills were unneces-sary or optional. When you have a passionate objective, you are in fact driven to acquire skill, since without it you can't satisfy your heart's desire. That's a far more powerful motivator than money alone can ever be.

To acquire skills, far too many people see merely one path: school or some sort of similar educational program. But this mass-market technique for skill development leaves you no better off than an army of others. Or people accept the same progression of experience that others have followed and, like sheep, move along. To their credit, Heather, Trent, and Ricardo looked more critically at their alternatives. They did not make mistake #3 of following the herd.

Heather decided that her accounting program had already given her most of the quantitative skills she needed to get an analyst job. A few more specialized courses were all that she needed to supplement them. As she investigated possible occupations where her quantitative analysis skills were in demand, she happened upon management consulting. As an accountant, she had a credible shot at getting a junior position. But a credible shot was not something that appealed to her planning zeal. She wanted an edge, especially because someone (can't imagine who) had terrified her about the highly competitive pressures of the modern economy.

So she sought out a retired consultant who had worked at a major firm and interrogated him. Heather learned that competition for clients among the big firms was intense, and the ability to find and retain key clients was much prized. That's all Heather needed to know. "Show me how to do that," she said. She cleverly and truthfully told him that he should not let his business experience go to waste. Heather made herself into his apprentice, retired though he was.

Trent had a different skills problem. He wanted to be a productivity consultant, a subset of management consultants. So unless he wanted to age and grow into having these responsibilities, his undergraduate education in business had to be added to with a graduate degree. The logical choice was to get an MBA. However, sensitive to the fact that many MBAs graduate every year and that many management consultants have MBAs, Trent was not confident that this additional degree would give him distinction. (Again, getting an MBA is an excellent step to a great career, but it depends on your goals and circumstances.)

Trent thought, *If I want to be a high-level productivity expert, I'd better find a specialized graduate program.* Alas, no such program could be found. Looking is always better than not looking, but looking doesn't guarantee you'll find anything useful. But Trent didn't give up or take the "easy" path, which would have been to get his MBA anyway. Instead, he became creative. He began to look for a graduate program where he would be allowed to do research into productivity tools. In other words, he would be able to serve his own purposes, with help from the educational institution.

Ricardo approached his skills deficiency differently. He had read himself into considerable competence, but he knew he lacked hands-on experience. In particular, Ricardo felt he needed to better understand financing. He thought about finding a mentor, but he wanted to start his new project right away. And time was short. So Ricardo decided to improvise, but in a planned way; he would hire professionals to work on his project, and learn skills from them as he went.

At this stage, Heather, Trent, and Ricardo avoided a major mistake. Many people get an issue half right and then fail to press their advantage. Heather, for example, could have just had casual conversations with her mentor. Trent could have chosen any research degree to start, and Ricardo could have just improvised the acquisition of financing skills. Each, however, developed *a clear, precise plan* to build their skill base. (In other words, they established benchmarks, which we will go over in detail on page 145.) Heather and her mentor prepared a series of meetings and introductions to accomplish very specific objectives covering all aspects of high-impact analysis, including how to attract clients. Trent exhaustively researched his prospective grad programs, having developed a set of criteria. His new education was supposed to buy him entry to productivity consulting, and he was leaving nothing to chance. To ensure that his vision was supported by experience in execution, Ricardo outsourced as much of the work on his strip mall project as he could. And then he decided to supervise very carefully, principally to learn what his partners were doing and, by questioning them, to find out why they were doing it. In other words, Ricardo would mostly be learning, instead of supervising. Next time, he would be smarter, and eventually he would be able to supervise knowledgeably.

From this trio you can learn to ask yourself the most critical skills questions. What skills do you still need that you are lacking? How can you get them? How much time do you have to do so? Are you looking at nontraditional methods for acquiring these skills, or are you just following the conventional "wisdom"?

Put Your Team in Place

Career success is almost never a solo achievement. Yes, networking is important, but what I'm advocating is something that goes beyond the network as it is usually understood. Of all the people I have known who have struggled in their careers in spite of following their passions, the most common reason for their struggles is their inability to mobilize a team. Notice I said a *team*, not a network.

It doesn't matter what the nature of your work is, whether you're in a small organization or a large one, a tech company or a manufacturer. Even in the notoriously isolated high-tech world, loners will struggle. Yes, they will get a job with decent pay, but after a time, with increasing stress, highly talented people start to resent their lack of control over their jobs. More often than not, it's this lack of control that holds them back from having a truly great career, and yet they could have fixed this if they'd had a team in place. They feel — usually correctly — that their talent is being wasted. Ah, if only they weren't so scared of strangers!

What is the difference between a network and a team? A network of people you know, and who think of you in a positive way, is one of the pools from which you recruit your team. Unlike a network, which should be so big you cannot from memory recall all of its members, a team is small, cohesive, and ready and able to help you achieve your career goals. The network is merely available, but the team is on-call. And if you (wisely) integrate key life goals into your career plan, the team is also important to the achievement of the plan for your life. The team often includes people of varying connections to you — some family, friends, acquaintances, work-mates, and your own hired professionals. Your team helps you plan, create, and execute.

Heather had recruited her key mentor, but that was only her start. There was no way she could learn everything she needed to know about finding clients from a single person. If it were that easy, everyone would be doing it and she would have no advantage. Her mentor had advised her that she would have to practice, not just learn, what needed to be done. So Heather set to work. She hired a professional researcher to brief her on likely new markets. Another member of her team, a valued friend and neighbor, arranged for her to attend a key trade show that was closed to the public. Her grandfather, a retired executive, listened to her practice her pitches. Are you starting to see why Heather is a force to be reckoned with?

Trent's team was heavily skewed toward professors who could help him evaluate his various graduate school educational choices. In addition, a classmate connected him with a retired senior executive at a global manufacturer who would know which firms did the best work in productivity. Trent also read almost every recent paper on productivity and tried to get a personal interview with the authors who most interested him. In essence, he was still putting his core team in place. His most serious challenge was finding someone who could help him finance his university research. Otherwise, he'd be a prisoner of his supervisor's own funding constraints.

Ricardo was fortunate, since his oncoming construction project brought him into contact with a wide range of professionals, government officials, bankers, tenants, and trade contractors. He auditioned all of them for his team, and in doing so, tried to learn everything he could from them. He also paid his accountant to brief him on an ongoing basis. Team Ricardo was healthy and strong.

A team is not a group that will do your bidding. Rather, team members are in a relationship with you, and a relationship is never a one-way street. You're not a kid anymore, and no one's looking after you simply for the sake of looking after you. Make a case to people as to why it's good for *them* to join *your* team.

For instance, a mentor might be an employee of a corporation that one day might want to recruit you. Or think about how Heather approached her mentor — she knew he was eager to do something that tapped into all of his experience. From his end, he wanted to pay it forward, pay it into the future, where his experience would long outlive him. And Heather could also give him something back, which was her own unique, millennial's view of the world. There was much that Heather knew that her mentor did not, and her perspective was, at the very least, interesting to him.

Sometimes members of your team will be paid, like Ricardo's accountant, but money should not be the driver for most of your team members. It should be based upon relationship. Though Ricardo was paying contractors to do work for his project, he wasn't paying them to teach him—they did that for free, because they likely saw potential in Ricardo and could see a long-term working relationship with him. And who knows? Perhaps they even charged him the lower end of their fee. Stranger things have happened.

Heather, Trent, and Ricardo have completed some very heavy lifting in this chapter. We've seen them through the first critical steps in their career planning: they've decided where they want to go and what they can let go of. They've isolated the major obstacles to their goals and really probed them to make sure there was no give. They've strengthened the skills they knew they'd need, and they've put their teams in place. And yet there's more work to do. For now comes what is perhaps the most crucial part of their plan: finding the edge that will set them apart.

Hard Questions, Honest Answers

1. What is your particular destination?
2. How do you rank your priorities?
3. What barriers stand in your way? Are they firm or can you move around them?
4. Who is truly on your team? What are you offering them in return for their support?

SIX

Find Your Edge

THE AUTHOR J. K. ROWLING could have written a good book instead of a great one. But she wanted an innovative story and remained true to her artistic vision. She violated all the rules of kids' books, which at the time said that nothing should be too scary or too long, and that all the adults must be noble. As the whole world now knows, the strategy worked out quite well for her.

If all you can produce from your work is a *good* result, you're not generating a competitive response. You're no better than most everyone else. So why would you expect to get any special advantage? You have to develop an attribute beyond skill. This means you need to create solutions that are highly innovative, solutions that are found in few other places, if any.

Let's return to our trio, Heather, Trent, and Ricardo, and how they faced the issue of finding their edge. Heather did not immediately see why her mentor pushed her to figure out what her special insight was going to be. She couldn't just want to have an impact on important problems through numerical analysis. Was she going to use a mathematical technique no one else thought to use? Or was she going to find a source of data no one else had or used? How was she going to solve problems using exceptional techniques? Slowly she realized that he was pushing her to find a systemic advantage as a problem solver — that it was not enough just to be "smarter."

Heather was amazed that, for all the excitement surrounding quantitative analysis, the so-called big data, there was very little attention being paid to ensuring the *accuracy* of the source data or even its consistency over time. Heather found a way to greatly improve this quality, and she was offered an excellent position. She still didn't travel as much as she'd hoped, but it didn't seem to matter to her as much. And she made the most out of the traveling she did do (with a well-thought-out plan, naturally). Trent faced a different version of the same need. He intended to use a piece of research to launch his career as a productivity consultant. But that still left him trying to decide which important productivity problem he was going to solve, and where. And if it was important and still unsolved, then it must be very difficult to solve. Why did he think he could solve it? What was his truly special insight? What mistakes were others making that he could avoid?

With the help of the team he put together, Trent chose a graduate program with great flexibility and built a curriculum for himself that allowed him time to do extensive research. Also through his team, he found out about a grant opportunity and secured funding to research how to organize manufacturing supply chains more productively. After graduate school, he was hired by a firm specializing in productivity consulting, even though they typically recruited people with more experience. But they loved his ideas, and they gave him a shot. He loves his condo, which he is slowly filling with furniture, and from the little he tells me on the matter, it appears his social life is also going well.

Ricardo was already exploring his distinction, set off by his prodigious reading. He wanted to use unusual design details to create architecturally distinguished and affordable buildings. But since he was trying to move quickly, he had to avoid adding details that slowed construction unduly. He had his edge — that was the easy part. The challenge was that he needed to remain focused and committed to executing his creative vision quickly.

Ricardo's strip mall project was a success, and he now knows that he loves being a property developer.

What these three stories illustrate is that it isn't enough just to have a passion, or even a passion and a plan; you must also have a *defining distinction,* or an edge. And that distinction involves the skill of creativity 100 percent of the time.

Don't think you're creative? Think again. By the end of this chapter, you'll see not only how crucial creativity is, but how to bring it out in yourself.

Yolanda and Cliff: Imitate vs. Innovate

Yolanda was certain that being creative just wasn't her thing. And that's why what happened to her was entirely predictable.

Yolanda was, in many ways, a model employee. She loved her work as head of the human resources team in a growing company. She thoroughly enjoyed the challenge of matching the right person to the right job, and she derived great satisfaction from doing so. Yolanda was even very careful to provide helpful feedback to applicants who failed to be hired, so that they might improve their prospects. She was committed to her own professional development and that of her staff through training, conferences, and workshops.

It was therefore bitterly disappointing when she was terminated after being with the company for more than a decade. Her boss tried to explain his decision. He reminded her that she had been cautioned to correct a weakness in her performance, and she had failed to do so. Out of respect for her years of service, he offered her a good reference, which omitted the actual reason she had been let go. That was small consolation for Yolanda, who still seemed not to understand what had happened to her.

So what had cost Yolanda her job? If you think she was a model employee, she was — but for the year 1980.

Here's what went wrong: Yolanda's employer was an up-and-coming company in a very competitive marketplace, and they believed that the quality of their employees was essential to maintaining their momentum. But over the past several years, the company felt that their competitors had been hiring better-quality employees than they had. Yolanda had been asked to improve their hiring and staff-retention strategies. But her efforts had been judged inadequate, since all she had done was duplicate the policies and programs of the other companies. When criticized, she had protested, saying that she had implemented HR industry best practices. *What more did they want?* she wondered. A lot more, it turns out.

By merely *matching* the best practices of her employer's competitors, Yolanda had provided no real competitive advantage. And that advantage is exactly what the company wanted and needed, especially since they hadn't been around as long as some of the competition. Competitive advantage meant creating and adopting recruitment and retention practices no one else was using. As a result, when Yolanda used a technique she learned about from a conference, she was still just imitating, not innovating. In times past, Yolanda's approach would have been good enough for her employer to withstand competition. But unfortunately, we are no longer in an era of "good enough."

All of Yolanda's training had been to recognize the smart ideas of others and to implement them appropriately. But here's the problem: That's the same training that armies of other college-educated HR professionals have had. In an age of rising standards, more is needed: longer hours, faster work, fewer mistakes. And still the competitive pressure mounts, for now we also need: new answers, better answers, and more innovative answers. Yolanda did not know how to deliver that standard.

Neither did Cliff, and he was on the edge of panic, fearing a recently won promotion would slip through his fingers. An engineer in love with engineering, he had developed a reputation in his company for his high level of technical proficiency. When given a problem, he typically applied his wealth of knowledge to deliver an effective solution at reasonable cost. As a result of his consistent track record, he was made assistant head of research and development. His first task was to lead a team to create a game-changing new product. Alas, the team's initial meeting was a disaster. The team looked to him for leadership and he looked to them for ideas. And both he and they quickly lost confidence in each other.

Yolanda and Cliff struggled because their employers were under competitive pressure. Simply working harder, faster, or longer would not address their employers' need for a competitive advantage. Cliff needed to innovate to hold on to his job. And Yolanda wasn't sure what she needed to do to get another job. How did Yolanda and Cliff get themselves into this position? Remember, both are very much pursuing their passions.

The problem was that they had assumed that their passion, education, and experience were all that were necessary. And it would have been — in the past. When I pressed them, both acknowledged that competition was increasing and that it was likely to continue increasing indefinitely. They also agreed that the workplace was going to keep getting more challenging.

But despite recognizing all this, they did not take it a step farther. They did not try to define the consequences of what they already knew was happening and then address those consequences. Since Yolanda and Cliff are alert and ambitious, their failure to worry about what the future held may seem somewhat surprising . . . until you realize the main issue affecting them both.

The Villain: Conventional Thought

Yolanda and Cliff were pursuing their passions, but in every other aspect of their lives they were bound to standard convention. They were strongly affected by their families, friends, and workmates, who toed the line and stayed safely within the norm—do your work, do it well, come home, go do it again. But thinking about the future in a methodical way is definitely not a herd exercise. As Cliff said, "The future seems kind of scary." Yes, if you ignore the future it certainly can scare you. And both Cliff and Yolanda were scared now.

Cliff was now ready to get serious about how to innovate. He didn't have a lot of time before his job self-destructed, and he knew it.

Yolanda, however, was still in denial. Well, sort of. She saw the logic behind my advice that she needed to innovate, but she'd already lost her job. "Maybe," she said hesitantly, "I can get my next job based on my experience. Then, sure, after I'm hired, I'll probably need to learn to innovate . . . I mean, *eventually*."

"You seem reluctant," I noted.

"Professor," she said, "I'm just not creative."

Conventional thought was paralyzing Yolanda. She assumed she would be unsuccessful at adapting, and so she didn't try to. She thought, even hoped, it would still all work out somehow.

I hate conventional thought. It sits—*lurks,* even—in the background, and it shapes your ideas without revealing itself explicitly, thus making it extremely powerful. I see it as a villain in the night, determined to subvert human talent. Again and again, I've seen this villain waste people's potential. *Toe the line; Follow the leader; If it ain't broke, don't fix it* — all are examples of conventional thought hiding within clichés. Of course, conventional ideas do change over time, but progress is slow. And in the time it usually takes to change them, we are collectively set back. A year wasted is a year lost forever, never to be regained. And as the drumbeat of competition increases, conventional thought lags behind reality by ever greater degrees.

In short, I saw Yolanda and Cliff becalmed in an ocean of conventionality, and they were drifting toward the rocks. They both felt that innovating was the job of the boss, whether they admitted it or not. That's a dangerous assumption to make. The herd tells itself that creativity is only for the special few — those rare individuals who can think up new stuff are true geniuses or weird anomalies. This tends to be a brilliant excuse for most people to avoid even an attempt at innovation: Most people *don't* innovate, ergo, they *can't!* If we need a solution to a problem, we solve it using yesterday's ideas, or we wait for the boss to find a solution. As a result, are you surprised that so many struggle in their careers?

So how was I going to liberate Yolanda and Cliff from conventionality? There are never easy answers when important issues are on the table. And the full realization of talent is, for me, of the utmost importance. It is the prize truly worth fighting for.

Understanding Innovation

Yolanda and Cliff needed to think about innovation and its companion, creativity, *a lot*. And given their conventional views, there was much for them to learn.

First, they needed to define *creativity*. When Yolanda insisted she was not creative, I asked what that meant. She said she had no artistic ability at all. By art, she meant the visual, dramatic, and musical arts.

"And what does that possibly have to do with innovation in HR processes?" I asked.

"If I have no artistic ability, I can't create anything new."

She had no evidence for that assertion. Clearly, she had not seriously thought about innovation. Art wasn't her passion; HR was. Why would one be connected to the other? The only reason to worry about artistic creativity is if you want to be an artist. Yolanda needed to be innovative in HR. She needed to understand everything about that specific kind of innovation.

While reading one of the many books about the process of innovation can be useful, I suggested as a first priority that both Yolanda and Cliff read about the last century's innovations in their respective fields. They needed to know what the innovations were exactly. How were they created? What caused them to succeed or fail? Who typically created them? As an unemployed job-seeker, Yolanda now had some time available to do what she should have been doing for years already. But she was now starting, at least.

Cliff felt under much more pressure, since his employer was still waiting for action, or at a least a plan of action. Determined to hold on to his promotion, Cliff threw himself into reading about innovations in his field of electrical engineering. He was now starting to understand the kind of innovation he cared about. He found his reading of great interest and admitted that in the past, while he had read a little about recent innovations, he had been neither particularly methodical nor analytical. "If only I had more time," he said wearily.

In spite of Yolanda's skepticism and Cliff's anxiety, they both had a powerful competitive edge. They loved their work and the subject of their reading was inherently interesting. Yolanda actually said it was fascinating, as she noted that most of what she was reading was unknown to her. Imagine how difficult it would be to do this kind of extensive reading if you did *not* find the subject interesting, if it wasn't your passion!

I have watched too many people try to create innovations in fields that the crowd tells them are hot. We talk. They want me to suggest a single perfect book for their needs. They usually say it's because they don't have a lot of time. Perhaps. But I suspect they see the reading as grinding, hard work. And I rarely see such persons develop anything new other than minor iterations of what others have already created.

It took Yolanda longer than Cliff to identify the innovations that had happened in her field. But find them she did. She learned about the workplace of the early twentieth century, where the rule of the day was "command and control." She learned how the psychological testing of job applicants had evolved, why skills-based testing had failed in many applications, and how the use of social media had grown quickly to recruit and evaluate candidates. And that was just a sample of what she'd learned. But what to do with all this research still stymied her. She needed to identify a current-day problem or issue in HR.

What Is Your Problem?

With Yolanda's knowledge of and passion for HR, she was gradually able to identify a number of key HR problems: How to recruit talent? How to retain talent? How to grow talent? Yolanda also saw that she needed to break down these big problems into smaller components. Under recruitment, there were the associated problems of identifying who you want, finding them, getting them to listen to your message, understanding what exactly they want, and verifying their credentials and references. She now had to figure out how to rank the importance of these problems. For example, where was the biggest failure, since fixing it would produce the biggest benefit for the employer?

Cliff had made little progress on the problem-identification side. He struggled with understanding exactly what his employer had meant by a "game-changing" new product. Cliff would have been so happy if the employer had just said to make a specific product cheaper, whereas "game-changing" seemed to be about a big market hit. And markets relevant to his employer were not something Cliff thought about a lot.

He was completely honest with me about it, actually — he said he never thought about it. That was the job of his boss, he figured. But this promotion, which he had wanted badly and actively sought, made him a "junior" boss. And as a boss-in-training, he was still in trouble. Desperate, he privately hired a consultant to help him identify key problems; he paid for this advice himself. He found a good consultant who knew how to ask questions. Cliff had always been good at identifying technical problems, but now he was tutored in identifying business problems.

First, Cliff needed to look at which products were slow sellers and why. What category of products close to the company's offerings was growing rapidly? The consultant showed him how to look. Cliff couldn't afford to have the consultant to do all the actual work, but his guidance showed Cliff which characteristics might qualify as game changers.

Cliff was now barely sleeping. Pressure and brutal hours are what awaits those who delay their own adjustments to the new realities of the marketplace. But Cliff managed to find at least a plausible game changer. His company had a low-selling product that would have been extremely useful to a much larger market, but it was far too expensive. If Cliff and his team could lower the cost of manufacturing dramatically, they should have a killer new product. Now Cliff needed to make this innovation happen.

What's Your Solution?

Yolanda hit the ground running, although at the same time she was very annoyed with herself. You see, years ago she'd thought of a solution to the problem of how to recruit the best talent, but she had given it no further thought.

"Why did you just shelve the idea back then?" I asked.

"I don't know," she said. "Maybe I just got too comfortable in my job. I remember worrying at the time that it might not work."

"And then what would have happened?" I asked. "Would you have gotten fired?"

Yolanda took the jab with good humor. It didn't matter anymore — Yolanda was on the march. She had game.

Yolanda had the basic idea of her innovation in her head, but she needed a working prototype, since it included a software component. She consulted her team of advisors, who had already rallied around her in the aftermath of her termination. She networked to add a software expert to her unpaid team. A friend of a friend later, Yolanda had a working prototype. There was still a lot of development work to do, but she could now prove that her idea worked.

Yolanda reoriented her job search, offering herself, her experience, and now her ideas for how to improve recruitment. Yolanda ended up with more than one offer. In her new job, Yolanda was determined that once she'd implemented her recruitment innovation, she'd move on to the next improvement. She had learned how essential that was.

Cliff was having less success. Every solution he came up with was just a version of a product that already existed and was still far too expensive. Cliff was so conditioned to using the textbook recipe instructions to solve problems that being original and creative seemed beyond him. And his team, whose conditioning matched his, was equally at a loss. What to do?

Cliff just kept at it. He encouraged his team to analyze their problem yet again. Was there a component in the product that could be eliminated? No. Was there an expensive component that could be redesigned to be cheaper? No. Could some of the features be eliminated? No, all were valued by the customers. Could a technology be moved from another application to Cliff's product? No. Nothing appeared relevant. He led his team in a brainstorming session and also tried to identify any mistakes that they or other companies had made with regard to the product. Were there untested assumptions that would offer them insight? Nothing stuck. Cliff confided that he wondered whether he was just too unimaginative to dream up an important innovation.

I urged Cliff to be patient and to persist. He was under an enormous amount of stress, and the challenge looked insurmountable. Of course he had moments of questioning himself—that's only natural. But he was forgetting that innovation is not meant to be easy. If it were, where would the competitive advantage be? I reminded him that innovation was a practiced skill, and that he had only just begun to practice. That made sense to him; as an amateur-ranked tennis player, he understood the value of practice. But he also had to practice that elusive skill of knowing when to quit one idea and to move on to another one.

Then, while Cliff was commuting home one evening, the confluence of persistence, inspiration, and a critical mass of information came together. This was not lightning striking—this was information congealing. Building on the work of his team, Cliff noticed that the original product design had been done for a select group of large, deep-pocketed, elite customers. Restraining cost had not been important. And that was the real problem: the entire design was inherently expensive. He and his team had been trying to modify the basic design to a lower cost. And *that* is why it proved to be a lost cause.

But if the team completely disregarded the original design and started from scratch, they could imagine a completely different approach to a product that would meet the same purpose as the expensive one. By the time Cliff reached home, he'd thought of several alternative low-cost technologies he could use. The bottom line? Cliff kept his promotion.

"But Professor . . .": Common Excuses to Innovation

I recognize that having to innovate for career success is intimidating to those who haven't yet done it. And I am frequently told when I make this argument to innovate that there are exceptions to it. Such as:

"But my employer doesn't want me to innovate!"
I believe students when they tell me this. I believe it because I see it all the time. One employer told an employee who was making a suggestion for an improvement, "That's not your job." (A direct quote!) On the contrary, suggestions for innovation are not annoyances or signs of arrogance, they are a necessity. People who came of age in a time when innovation was not as crucial as it is today don't always value it — they don't do it, and they can even feel threatened by those who encourage it. I have watched law firms flounder because they believed that courting new clients was be-

neath them; I have watched behemoth corporations like General Motors fail because they did not see and value the change around them.

So can you guess what I tell students who come to me and say their company has a real lack of regard for innovation? I tell them, of course, it's time to find another employer. Get out ahead of a termination, because that employer will not survive. In the end, it doesn't matter what the employer or employee wants, it's the marketplace that will ultimately decide, and in a competitive economy, only those firms that innovate will survive.

"But I work in a helping profession — social work — innovation doesn't apply to me."

The great company of teachers, healthcare workers, social workers, and counselors of every kind are often cited as exceptions to the innovation rule. For these occupations, people feel they need only competence in their field, communication skills, and empathy. But are they really exempt from the dictates of competition?

Consider Helen, a nurse in a major medical facility. She loves her work, is well trained, and enjoys the profound satisfaction of helping patients return to health or achieve the best quality of life possible. However, Helen faces severe workload pressure from the increasingly complex needs of her patients, from ever-expanding treatment options, and from hospital management that is trying to rein in the relentlessly rising cost of healthcare. All the nurses strenuously complain about the shortage of staff and the risks associated with what they see as understaffing.

Helen, fiercely committed to her patients' well-being, didn't just complain — she took action. She started proposing changes in workplace practices and in facilities, all to reduce the low-value work she and her colleagues found themselves performing. She developed a better tracking system to avoid patient distress before it occurred. Helen attracted attention to herself by doing so. When the position of head nurse in her unit became available, the most experienced nurse who had long advocated for more resources (from a resource-constrained organization, remember) applied for the job. In times past, the job would have been hers almost automatically. The job went to Helen instead. The more experienced nurse was bitterly disappointed, and I felt sorry for her. She had no idea what had happened, but she was out of her place in the slipstream of time. Helen, meanwhile, will undoubtedly become the hospital's director of nursing one day. Helen clearly understood the need for innovative solutions in the hospital, and she knew how to implement them.

And then there is Bruce, a highly committed mental health counselor who deals with suicidal youth. It would be difficult to express his passion and dedication for preventing the deaths of young people by their own hand. By the time I met Bruce, he'd long exerted every ounce of his training and experience to help those who fell under his care. But Bruce did not always succeed, and he felt each loss personally. Indeed, Bruce's family became concerned for his own mental well-being in such a harrowing and demanding job. I asked him why he wasn't trying to innovate. His first reaction to that suggestion was to dismiss it, that it was crazy. Then he thought about it some more and started to wonder the same thing.

His supervisor had once told him, "We can't win them all. We just try as hard as we can." Suddenly, what had been comforting words now sounded hollow. *Maybe we can't win them all,* he thought, *but we need to find better ways to help.* That involved more than trying as hard as he could. That meant finding better ways to do his job. So Bruce became an aggressive innovator. Dissatisfied with the initial screening tool used to identify high-risk youth, he developed his own screening techniques and began the research protocol necessary to validate them.

Can those in the helping professions really believe that there can't be improvements at every level? Teaching? Healthcare? Counseling? And if you are in the helping professions or want to enter them, why would you think that the improvements must always come from others? Don't you often complain that the new tools you are given do not work well because some ivory-tower academic created them? Would it not be more logical that the frontline worker is best positioned to create practical innovations to improve service? Too many talented people simply wait for others to take action. What an odd response for those who say they are committed to helping others. Apparently, that commitment does not extend to innovating in order to help. Have I struck a nerve? I'm not sorry — my intent was to light a fire in your mind.

"But you're clearly picking exceptional examples, Professor. Most people can't create tools like Helen and Yolanda, or have great breakthroughs like Cliff did."

I'll acknowledge that the stories I've told in this chapter are about people who are not average workers. But remember, we are talking about *great* careers, not average ones. And if you suppose that these constitute a very small handful of examples I know of, then you are mistaken. They're not the majority yet, but their numbers grow all the time. As they do, more and more organizations will adopt the expectation for "exceptional."

Indeed, I know people who have sped up their careers and served society by delivering innovation across the widest range of work and industries. There are those whose innovations increased the pace of corporate processes; those who eliminated entire functions (and some of their fellow workmates); those who found new markets or reinvigorated mature ones; those who lowered costs or drove up productivity; those who increased the likelihood of success in delivering social services; those who developed entirely new product categories; those who pioneered new marketing techniques; those who created new dramatic art; those who created new professional services; and those who brought insight where before there was confusion. The truth is, my problem when planning this chapter was one of having too many examples to share, not a shortage of them. But all of these stories have one common theme: innovation got these people ahead.

Why am I so sure that you can innovate? Because I've seen so many men and women from widely different backgrounds do so very successfully, and then go on to use those innovations to craft great careers.

To Sum Up on Innovation . . .

Let's be clear: Being an innovator is difficult work. It takes time to prepare and to execute an idea, and it involves no small amount of frustration. I can't give you all the answers you need to innovate in your field because I don't know your field. But you do. Or you should — you should know it backward and forward. You need to know everything about it to understand what it is still lacking.

In addition to reading and putting careful thought into your future, I'm telling you to do something else, as well: to dust off and reactivate your rusty imagination, last used when you were around nine years old. Remember when you looked around your room to determine what materials could make a suitable fort? It's that same creativity, the same imagination you need now.

Imagining is not a fast process in a world that celebrates quick results (in fact, it demands even more work). This is why you will need to manage your time carefully. You will need to be disciplined to avoid distractions and to maintain your focus. But you have seen the word *discipline* in this book before. And the fact that you are still here with me tells me you believe in the importance of discipline. You are already ahead of most.

Hard Questions, Honest Answers

1. What is your unique distinction?
2. How are you tapping into your creativity?
3. What problem can you help your employer solve? How?

SEVEN

Sell Yourself by Selling Your Idea

KNOW, I KNOW. A bad taste just filled your mouth at the idea of pitching yourself. Sadly, too many people seem to recoil at the concept of having to go out in the real world and sell themselves or their ideas.

But again, we're being realistic, remember? And the truth is that *all the other steps are in vain unless you can mount an effective marketing campaign for yourself.* The good news is that you don't have to say, "I am so great! Look at me!" but instead you can say, "I have some great ideas — what do think about these?" *Because if a person or company loves your ideas, they will want you.*

You must be able to deploy all your preparations and to define what distinguishes you. The world needs to know why you are different, and why this difference makes you highly valuable. This message must be clearly defined and sustained throughout your entire career. Such marketing is essential, whether you are just starting out, like Heather and Trent, or you're changing careers, like Ricardo.

Self-marketing is equally important for the advancement of an ongoing career. Too many people create an effective career plan that lands them an excellent opportunity, but then they let the planning lapse on the crazy assumption that, although the job came from the plan, the promotion will be automatic. In the past, maybe that was true, but no more. Remember that your plan is for your overall career success, not just for getting a job.

Banish the "Ick" Factor

The first thing we need to deal with is the fear of selling yourself and your ideas.

Though we live in a world of selfies and self-promotion, the truth is that most people feel uncomfortable blatantly selling themselves in personal encounters. Somehow, they find it demeaning. A friend told me one of the saddest sights she'd ever seen was a man in a vampire costume at a book show, giving out free copies of a vampire novel he'd written. "It was beyond depressing," she said. "No one wanted to even make eye contact with the guy — we all felt he was embarrassing himself in his desperation to be noticed."

Then there are those who have a product they're trying to sell you, and they do so with such vigor that even as you try to pass them by on the street or hang up the telephone, they make it impossible for you not to appear rude. These are horrible examples of salesmanship, and anyone who would consider selling their ideas in such a way would be well advised to improve their judgment before anything else.

In other words: don't worry. I am not going to advise you to take extreme measures like these. Quite the contrary. Marketing yourself — convincing others of your value — is more of a subtle art, and one that can be mastered without being obnoxious or wearing vampire teeth.

Define Yourself, or Someone Will Do It for You

Bart was a passionate landscape gardener whose creations were mystically beautiful. His customers routinely described his work as exceptional, amazing, brilliant, and never-seen-anything-like-it. But he had a big problem. His creations were typically very expensive, and he soon exhausted his pool of local clients. Furthermore, he was so good that no one wanted to change their gardens after he was finished. In other words, he had few repeat customers.

Bart, however, was smart, and he decided to innovate. He started to use less-expensive materials and plants to lower his costs and expand his market. Unfortunately, he was known as the rich person's gardener, and the few ads he placed in local publications brought in only a handful of leads. And even then, when he met a prospective new client, he had trouble closing a sale.

I'd known Bart for years, and he came to see me to discuss what was going wrong. He was passionate and skilled, and his new, less costly gardens seemed even more striking than the previous versions he'd designed. But he was stuck with the distinction he'd earned by default. He'd never wanted to be the gardener to the rich. When I asked him whose gardener he wanted to be, he said, "I want to be the gardener of those who value the disciplined beauty of richly varied plants and blooms." His eyes got a faraway look that showed me just how much he loved his work — he was clearly envisioning gardens as we spoke.

But the customer Bart wanted was not the customer his reputation attracted. He was trapped in the wrong identity, and it was limiting both his artistic freedom and his income. Bart worried he might have to uproot his family and start anew in another community, where his reputation wasn't known.

Bart needed to take initiative and redefine his professional image. It would have been better, obviously, if he'd defined himself as he wished to be known from the beginning, instead of getting rid of one image and then building another. And to make an already challenging task more challenging, he was very clear that he did not want to be a salesperson.

"Why are you so reluctant to sell yourself and your design innovations?" I asked him. "Could it be that you don't believe in your own capability, or the quality of your ideas?"

"That's not it at all," Bart insisted. "I just don't want people to think I'm a huckster. I mean, nobody likes a salesperson."

Well, perhaps *Bart* didn't like salespeople. And I'll acknowledge that no one likes the pushy telemarketing call. But millions do look to sales professionals for guidance about everything from cars to electronics to cosmetics. Bart was right to make sure he wasn't confused with a disreputable sales scammer, but I suspected there was more to his reluctance than that.

Slowly, it became clear that the huckster problem was a convenient cover for Bart's shyness. His shyness was not immediately obvious, because he wasn't an antisocial loner; he was married and had a community of good friends. But in a group of strangers — such as potential clients — he was plainly uneasy. After he got to know someone, he became comfortable, but it took him a relatively long time. So how could this naturally quiet person become an effective advocate for himself? Or was Bart forever at a disadvantage because of his shy personality?

I fully accept that Bart, and many others like him, are at some disadvantage in promoting their ideas. But he should nevertheless try; his personality is not an excuse for going bankrupt. I'm not suggesting that he undergo a radical personality transplant — he's not going to run for mayor or become the life of the party every time he enters a room. But the fact is that all of us, in some way or other, are going to have to leave familiar turf if we're going to have a great career. Your trusty professor, a shy country boy, had to. And it might well turn out that what Bart thinks is an immutable personality characteristic isn't.

"But Professor," I often hear, "I have to be true to myself. I am who I am." People say this to me all the time when I encourage them to step out of their comfort zones. But it's never that simple. If Bart was going to be true to himself, he also had to be true to the expression of his talent. So which truth had to yield? The truth of his talent or the truth of his shyness?

That was the sharp-edged choice Bart had to face. I bluntly asked him, "When you die, do you want your family and your community to remember that you were shy . . . or do you want them to remember your gardens?" Bart did not take more than a moment to decide that it was his gardens. As I said, beautiful gardens were his passion. And his passion gave him courage. (Imagine how stressful it would be for you to sell yourself if you were shy *and* you had no emotional attachment to the product of your work! Ever wonder why so much of sales seems insincere? That's because it is.)

Bart saw the wisdom of breaking out of his comfort zone. Nevertheless, he was daunted by the task ahead of him, and it was a big one. But his story also shows a clear silver lining: There are many ways to define and to market your work. It won't be easy, but Bart could at least choose what his distinction would be.

I will come back to Bart's predicament later in the chapter so you can see how he found the solution to overcoming his shyness and reluctance to sell himself.

Defining Yourself with Your Words

"Words are shallow," said my former student Stanley. "Marketing is just spinning words to confuse or manipulate people." I couldn't deny that yes, that's sometimes true. But not always.

Unfortunately, many of us have little experience in expressing ourselves about ourselves. This lack of practice greatly limits the interview skills of job applicants, whose career prospects plummet right out of the gate. They know they have to present themselves well, of course. They know about dressing appropriately. Shaking hands firmly. There are no spelling mistakes on their résumés, which must follow a standard format. They know to ask sensible questions about their potential job duties. The result? An army of clones saying almost the same thing, with almost no apparent conviction or passion.

Stanley was one of those who followed this pedestrian model, even though he cared deeply about his career as a chef and was uncommonly innovative. But he didn't show enough respect for the power of words, and he unintentionally presented himself as a soldier chef—one of the many who graduated from professional cooking schools. He said nothing interesting about himself or cooking. He had a résumé with an impressive culinary certification and a few cooking jobs, and he decided to let that speak for him.

Stanley came to see me when he was laboring as a cook in the institutional kitchen of a global hospitality company. After preparing the same meal for what seemed like the millionth time, he was crushed by boredom. He asked for "a few tips" to look for a better job. He was incredibly frustrated, for he had many ideas about how to prepare new kinds of dishes, ideas he'd been given no opportunity to try out. Who asks the common soldier to lead the army into battle, except in the movies? Stanley was now ready to respect and to accept the power of words. Without taking this step, he feared his career was running into a dead end.

Remember this: Words define you to the world *and* to yourself. I've listened to hundreds of talented men and women try — but fail — to tell me about themselves, their interests, and their goals. Even when I ask lots of pointed questions, their responses wander far and wide, without reaching any destination. When you have to express your talent in a few words, you discover how very difficult it is. So let's take it step by step.

The Elevator Pitch: Brief, Distinctive, and Enticing

The phrase *elevator pitch* originated among startup investors who insisted that entrepreneurs should be able to describe their ventures in the fifteen seconds it takes for a typical elevator ride. In other words, you should be able to describe yourself and your idea in just a few sentences, so that no matter how casual the occasion, you can "pitch" yourself. The goal is to leave no marketing opportunity wasted.

Sound too aggressive? Sound like you are supposed to always be in pitch mode? Are you rolling your eyes because you think this approach is what's wrong with the world? Well, this ever-alert-to-opportunity stance is the natural consequence of our world's competitive pressures. If you need a refresher on those pressures, go back and read chapter 1 again.

"But I don't want to be an entrepreneur," many students insist when I tell them about the elevator pitch. "I just want a great job."

Ah, but you are an entrepreneur. And your venture is yourself — it's a venture that has to be defined, polished, and marketed. The truth is, successful ventures and successful careers are much closer together than you might have thought. So put your startup face on, and let's learn how to pitch yourself.

Violet was a passionate art historian. There seemed to be absolutely nothing that she did not find interesting about her field. She was fascinated by its larger-than-life personalities, the underlying technologies of art, the historical context, the social impact, and the metaphorical interpretation, to name only parts of her interests. (I learned to never ask about specific things, like fresco painting techniques, because she would answer me . . . at great length.) She spoke with enthusiasm, and a conversation with her about art could be both stimulating and exhausting. Notwithstanding all of this, she had never really defined herself. And as a result, her career was stalled.

Violet had plenty of words to say; they just weren't the right ones or framed in the right way. She was still at the first job she had secured after graduation — working as a part-time curator in a reputable art gallery. But, though she'd been there for four years already, it did not look like she would get promoted anytime soon, and she had not gotten any of the jobs she'd applied for at other galleries. Actually, she was only rarely even getting an interview. The gallery world was closely knit, and Violet attended every event she could, where she thought she networked effectively. In short, Violet didn't understand what the problem was. She'd even taken to carrying a compact mirror with her at all times and compulsively checking her teeth — perhaps she had a tendency to get food stuck in them, and that was the issue.

To uncover the problem, I asked Violet for her fifteen-second elevator pitch. What I got was a four-paragraph sermonette, and even then I had to stop her. It was no wonder her networking opportunities weren't fruitful, and it had nothing to do with her teeth.

It's not that Violet should just say, "Hello, I'm Violet, an art historian." That's a greeting, not a pitch. The goal of the pitch is to invite further dialogue, dialogue with a purpose. But first she had to evoke interest. So, first I suggested that she should stop telling others why art was interesting to her; instead, Violet needed to interest the person she was talking to in Violet. That meant speaking to the *listener's* needs, not her own. And for those of you who think marketing is inherently sleazy, please notice that you start by focusing on others, not yourself.

"Tell me," I said, "how your passion can help others."

"Which others?"

"Others who need your help," I replied. "Is that people who buy art? People who run galleries? People who go to galleries? All of the above?"

"Yes, all of them . . . I could define myself as someone who helps collectors buy quality art," she suggested.

"Better," I said. "But far from distinctive. Don't many — if not most — art consultants make the same pitch? You need a sharper definition, a special innovative insight. Or," I added lightly, "are you just competent?"

Violet glared at me. She knew that by suggesting she was merely competent, I was damning her with faint praise. "No!" she said. "You know that, Professor! I'm much more than competent!"

"How so?" I asked.

"Because," she said quickly, "I take a much more comprehensive view of art than most so-called experts." Then, in her exasperation with me, I could see the lights begin to go on. "I could say I identify new artists that others miss —"

"Stop," I advised. "That is the basis of your pitch." Violet needed to be aware of her tendency to run on, and she had to know to pull back once she'd laid her hook in simple terms. Let the other person *ask* how you do it.

Notice now the characteristics of Violet's pitch:

1. Short
2. Distinctive ("I do something others do not.")
3. Expressed in a way that invites the listener to ask for more information

Let's unpack these three items a bit. Before Violet could describe her talent succinctly, she first had to figure out what it was. She needed to decide what was important to share and what wasn't. She had to strip her talent down to its essential elements, refined in the fire of brevity. Most critically of all, she could not take cover in a comfortable embrace of generalities. The best elevator pitch for Violet was simply, "I identify new artists that others miss." It was perfect.

This is one of the best rules of communication: let the other person ask before you provide an answer. It might then mean that the listener is . . . well, actually listening.

The fear I hear a lot is, "But what if my interest doesn't match what an employer is looking for? Isn't it safer to be more general, so that they can slot me in wherever they want?" Yes, you might fit *their* job, but it might not be *your* job, the job you should have, the job your talent demands.

Bart, too, had to create a pitch. He was very interested in the fifteen-seconds rule because he was more comfortable when he had to say fewer words. "I make beautiful gardens," he offered as a start.

"And that's a good contrast to your competitors?" I asked. "I suppose they say they make ugly gardens?"

"Oh, right," Bart laughed. "Good point."

"What kind of beauty is in your gardens?" I asked. Again, the goal is to define distinction by striking to the heart of the matter. Bart struggled a bit, because this man of few words knew what he meant but had never really put it into a short and precise pitch. He was truly of the old school, the very old school, back when your work spoke for you.

Bart was quiet for a long time, then he said, "I design gardens whose beauty is expressed in a thousand surprises."

It was a great pitch — it invited an obvious question: what kind of surprises? Again, a dialogue, a *relationship,* was now underway. Like Violet's, his pitch was short and intriguing, a baited hook, fishing for interest.

Bart and Violet now had pitches that were distinctive, not too general, and, importantly, not too narrow. Let me clarify a bit, because this is an important point. Imagine Violet's prospects if she'd said she loved the history of impressionist artists who worked in southern Italy from 1936 to 1940. Or do you think Bart would make progress if he said he loved French-style gardens with cherry trees and daisies? Probably not, but people say such things all the time. What if someone claims he wants to work with 3-D imaging for Disney, using classic cartoon characters in manga-style story format? That's an idea for a piece of work, and it might even be an innovative idea. But it is *not* a precise description of talent or its distinction. The goal is to be precise about the *body of work* you wish to create. Bart and Violet had a vision for this, and it would power their careers and set their direction.

Finally, note that Violet's and Bart's pitches are much more than just phony come-ons, for the simple reason that they are authentic and true. Violet really does study a multitude of factors to find overlooked artists, and she delivers results. And Bart's gardens are surprising in many ways, making them innovative. There is truth in advertising, which is the only way to succeed. You cannot build a great career on just hype.

The Follow-Up Paragraph: The Hook and the How

Having hooked the interest of their listeners, both Bart and Violet needed to create a script to handle the follow-up questions. Bart had to show how he infuses surprise into the very old art form of landscape gardening. And Violet had to explain how her comprehensive approach finds overlooked artists. They needed to see their scripts as a paragraph, not a chapter. Brevity is always a friend in a time-starved world.

Yet the first goal of the follow-up paragraph is actually not to answer the *how* question; it's to strengthen the hook. In fishing jargon, you jerk the line and pull the hook in so the fish cannot wriggle off. The same is true in networking/marketing sessions. The relationship between the person advancing an idea and the person listening to the argument is tenuous. So Bart, in response to the listener's vague expression of interest, needed first to solidify that interest, as did Violet. The best way to do that is to surprise the listener with a relevant fact, not an opinion. One of the fastest ways to impress anyone is to tell them something that's much different from what they would have assumed. Now *you* look interesting, not just your idea. The listener is implicitly wondering what other surprises will be revealed. Offer just one surprising fact, not a blizzard of them. Otherwise you will quickly look like an arrogant bore to be avoided like the plague. Bart didn't like talking to strangers, so he would do well in this regard. Violet, in contrast, would have to restrain herself, so enthusiastic was her style of speech.

Bart struggled with what his fact would be, and came to realize two important lessons. First, by trying to figure out what fact might surprise his listeners, he started to put himself in their place. This is exactly right. You do not win people over unless you can get into their minds. If you can figure out what will surprise them (or make them smile or frown), you will then see how they will respond to your entire argument.

Second, Bart saw that a surprising fact can often spark a creative insight. He grasped that his past customers liked having things in their gardens that others did not — they liked showing visitors new, unconventional plants. So Bart chose to open his paragraph with the observation that the average garden contained no more than 1 percent of all the plants that could conceivably be used. (He wasn't sure what the actual number was, but to his trained eye, that was a crude approximation. He decided he would find out for sure.) The clear implication — conveyed in only two sentences — is that Bart's designs use many types of plants. Let's look at the flow of Bart's script.

> LISTENER: And what do you do?
> BART: I'm a landscape gardener, and I specialize in gardens with hidden surprises.
> LISTENER: What kinds of surprises? How do you do that?
> BART: It's pretty straightforward, actually. I'm amazed that the average garden contains no more than one percent of all the plants that could be used. My gardens, by contrast, contain at least ten percent. Of course, I have to be very careful to make sure these highly varied plants complement each other.

(A word of caution: Never say "Did you know . . ." to anyone you are pitching yourself to. That sounds too much like one-upsmanship.)

The 10 percent benchmark came to Bart as he composed his script. Interesting, is it not, how necessity fuels good ideas? Bart was already thinking of plants he had never considered using.

Violet followed a similar approach and produced this script:

> LISTENER: So, what do you do?
> VIOLET: I'm an art consultant, and I love finding artists that others have missed.
> LISTENER: Really? Do you find overlooked artists very often?

VIOLET: Yes, quite often. It was quite a revelation to me that, of the century's top fifty artists, thirty of them became famous only after they were dead. But if you take a broad view, there are a lot of common elements to great art.

(When Violet and I worked on her script, she did not have the precise numbers, though she was eager to find them.)

The pitches are, of course, intended only to be relevant to a specific target; for Bart and Violet, they are directed to lovers of gardens and art only. Both Bart and Violet now had a dialogue underway with those potential clients. They could use slightly modified versions of their elevator pitches and follow-up paragraphs for networking events, job interviews, sales presentations, and even cocktail parties.

The One-Pager: Talking Points for Deeper Dialogue

Once you've hooked your listener and intrigued him with your fascinating fact and innovative distinction, it's time to drill down and drive it home. The one-pager is a series of talking points in which you deploy a few more interesting and important facts about your domain; the nature of your key innovation, with examples; and alternative ideas and suggestions for different groups of people. Make sure you actually write this part down. Obviously, you're not going to pull it out of your pocket or purse during a conversation and refer to it, but writing it all down will help you solidify, organize, and memorize your thoughts. Here's an example of what Violet's might look like:

Violet's One-Pager

- *Talk about Mitch O'Donnell and his crazy story of being discovered after doing artwork for his kids' school auction (people love this story!).*

- *Mention Gabriella, who I found right out of art school when I went and spoke to the school instructors and whose work is now worth hundreds of thousands of dollars.*
- *Talk about how other experts only read trade journals to find talent and overlook sources like Instagram or Pinterest.*
- *For more traditional clients: Definitely tell that story about how I brought hundreds to a gallery show by partnering with a revered winery.*

A common concern among those who have been on the receiving end of this advice is that following a script is going to sound artificial; they want to improvise. Unfortunately, they often later admit that their improvised conversations did not go all that well. In addition to forgetting a key point, they went off topic, found themselves in a conversational dead end, or repeated themselves three times.

It's true that the first time you practice your script, it will most likely sound wooden or artificial. And when you talk to someone like this for the first time, it will sound contrived, especially if you think you sound like me and not like yourself. But by the tenth time, you will, like magic, now sound like *you,* even though you're using the exact same words you used the previous nine times. Why? You just became accustomed to the sound of your own voice saying words that no longer feel new or awkward.

Remember this too: Words matter. Stanley, our chef, managed to put aside his preconceptions about marketing, and his results were quick and powerful. He introduced himself as "a chef who loves giving diners upscale presentations of comfort foods." He delighted in talking about how a buttermilk-fried chicken breast could be transformed by topping it with a celeriac purée, or how mac and cheese could be prepared with Dungeness crab and served in a small, Spanish-style cazuela. Not long after he'd implemented his new strategy, Stanley had a new job at a restaurant known for its innovative cuisine and willingness to take risks.

Defining Yourself with Your Actions

While the right words are critically important to define and to promote your distinctive talent, they are not enough. While well-crafted words describe what you can do, have done, or would like to do, *showing* someone what you have created is one of the most powerfully persuasive acts available. Its effect should not be underestimated. Yes, Bart should describe his vision for his garden of surprises, but nothing substitutes for showing a prospective client one of the gardens he has created — which he could do through postcards, business cards, his website, and even simply a snapshot on his phone, depending on the formality of the conversation. Bart is very comfortable in this space — he's long felt comfortable letting his work speak for him.

But what about Violet? What sample of her work could she show? Well, she could show the work of one of the overlooked artists she'd identified. She could lead a gallery tour demonstrating the hallmarks of great artists she has found. Both Bart and Violet have the advantage of working with visual, physically embodied products. And Stanley can always make someone a meal or show photos of his plating techniques.

As a lawyer seeking a job, Kylie didn't have these same advantages. What could she do? Draw up a sample contract? Sue someone for malpractice? She could easily use words to describe her unique insights, but how to *show* them? She felt passionately, for instance, that corporate bylaws could create humane and highly efficient workplaces. But no matter how eloquently Kylie spoke of these ideas, at her current job she was stuck drawing up routine contracts with a bewildering number of minor iterations.

In other words, no one wanted to give Kylie a shot based on her ideas. They needed real, tangible proof. And it makes sense; given the quantity of scammers, con artists, spin-masters, exaggerators, and wheelers and dealers, skepticism as a first reaction is warranted. While words are very important, they are also in many ways cheap. It is far easier to say that you will do something than to actually do it. So how could Kylie overcome this obstacle when no one would give her a chance?

In addition to skepticism, Kylie faced another foe: a culture that lacked imagination. This cultural lack is one of the most formidable obstacles to anyone pursuing a great career. Great careers are driven by the innovations that arise from passion. But such visions of what could be created are difficult for the unimaginative to grasp. (And that's part of the reason unimaginative people turn their backs on great careers.)

To fight both of these obstacles, Kylie needed a sample of her imaginative work. The problem? For some passionate careers, the nature of the sample is not immediately obvious.

Kylie struggled with this dilemma for some time. She wrote several papers for scholarly journals, spoke at conferences, and advocated her ideas before senior lawyers. There had been a few expressions of vague interest, but nothing really significant had occurred. Kylie was now not sure whether she should continue trying along these lines. Perhaps she should generate other ideas in a similar vein, but she felt she'd likely find herself in the same place.

Yes, Kylie could just keep trying, and over years she might succeed. In many cases, long persistence will pay off in great careers. But it's a riskier choice solely because it plays out over a longer period of time, where more things can change or go wrong. Surely it serves Kylie better to be successful sooner rather than later. And if she is successful sooner, Kylie will be even more creative over her lifetime, which serves everyone.

Kylie needed to apply her ingenuity to produce a sample of her vision. She needed to take action. As a practical matter, she needed to figure out what was the smallest realization of her idea but was still big enough to be persuasive. It took her some experimentation and a couple of dead ends, but finally she got it. She approached a small charity and volunteered to redraw their corporate bylaws to improve their operations. All Kylie asked in return was to be allowed to evaluate the effects of the new governance structure. She then repeated the process with a bigger charity, and finally she'd garnered the attention to her idea that she needed.

And finally, remember this: Every career direction and idea will require its own unique approach — there is no one-size-fits-all here. Yolanda, the HR professional we discussed in chapter 6, used her team to help her build a prototype. Helen, the nurse, prepared a plan to alter one aspect of her unit's workflow, and she implemented it unasked. You may recall that Ricardo, the property developer, completed a small project as a first step. Trent had his master's degree research as a sample of his ideas. On some occasions, it will be necessary to do this initial work speculatively, for no pay. Indeed, you might actually have to bear some direct expense to create your sample.

Notice the contrast between the typically unpaid internship and the samples of work discussed above. While the intern may deliver sample pieces of work, such samples are usually just in response to the request of the intern's supervisor and are no more than routine. But in our examples, the entire point is to demonstrate an innovation, not just competence. If only more interns recognized this possibility, it could make their presence felt!

• • •

I will be the first to admit that this segment of the book has recommended a challenging course of action. Even when you are working within the domain of your passion, creating an innovation is demanding and often frustrating. And still you're not done, since I've shown you that you need to marshal a full sales effort to advance your innovation. You need to fight whatever demons are preventing you from selling your vision. You need to determine how to define yourself with a pithy elevator pitch that will prompt your listener to ask more questions, then you need to be ready to expand that pitch into a paragraph, and finally into a full conversation. You need to be prepared to *show,* not just describe, your unique edge. And you must do all of this while making it seem like the most natural thing in the world. No problem. Oh, and then, once you've done all of this, you must do the immensely important work of actually executing your career plan, the subject of the next chapter.

Hard Questions, Honest Answers

1. What is your elevator pitch for your ideas?
2. What is your follow-up paragraph (the hook and the how)?
3. What is your one-pager? What different points will you emphasize, depending on the audience?
4. How do you plan to *show* the strength of your ideas?

EIGHT

Execute and Revise

NONE OF THE PLANNING PROCESS is effective if execution is not careful and sustained. Execution takes focus and hard work, and people are quick to offer excuses to abandon the effort altogether. The truth is, about half of the career plans I learn of are aborted before completion, or after a first job. And no one has ever given me a good reason as to *why* they've given up. (In the next section we'll delve into the excuses they give.)

Willingness to reevaluate your plan periodically and revise, if necessary, is just as important as strong execution. Be disciplined about your plan, but not so rigid that you cannot see room for improvement or be willing to change. An unexpected change in your plan does not mean quitting, tossing it out altogether. All plans change, and good ones can handle detours or even just bumps along the way. For instance, every plan should take into account what to do in case of a recession or layoffs. How will you revise your plan when the time comes? In many cases, my students don't ditch their plans at all but improvise some sort of temporary employment. Having a plan is what helps them maintain their longer-term focus while weathering what comes in the meantime.

The key to reevaluating your plan and assessing whether you need to revise is simple: *Create benchmarks.* These are the interim steps necessary for all the guidelines I've gone over in Part II of this book. How do you know your plan is actually working if you don't have benchmarks? You wouldn't set up a yearly budget without checking monthly to see how you're doing. Companies would never neglect to establish benchmarks, and your company of one shouldn't neglect this important step, either. As the saying goes, "If you can't measure it, you can't manage it." (But notice that in your process of reevaluation, you might conclude you have adopted the wrong benchmark.)

To better understand benchmarks, let's look at one of the strategies I discussed in chapter 5: Identify, Acquire, and Strengthen the Key Skills You Need. You can already clearly see that that's three to-dos, not one. But it's actually many more. If acquiring the skills you need involves attending graduate school, benchmarks could include researching the right programs and visiting prospective schools. And I'm still not done! Further benchmarks would be asking professors and current students questions in order to assess that school's suitability for you. Think about how many benchmarks you can include with each step in your plan. Set specific days that you will go over your benchmarks to gauge whether you are on track. Sometimes, that's how you'll notice that one of your steps won't work. Perhaps when you research the right programs, you learn that the best programs for you will take twice as long to complete as you'd anticipated. So revise your plan. Benchmark, review, revise, repeat. This is how you move forward.

Three Critical Questions

Logical though the preceding steps are (benchmark, review, revise, repeat), they are not easy to follow effectively. With the pace of today's economy, you must react quickly to a never-ending stream of new data. You must have constancy of purpose while at the same time exhibiting great flexibility at a tactical, execution level. In some ways, these two priorities are exact opposites of each other. Inability to balance the two causes many people to be reactive instead of thoughtful.

My student Nelson had done everything right. He had carefully identified his overriding passion — graphic design — and had developed a thoughtful plan to strengthen his innovative techniques and to market himself and his ideas. He knew he'd love to be an art director someday. Unfortunately, shortly after launching his plan, his career stalled — he didn't meet certain benchmarks (in his case, promotions) he'd set for his rise to his dream job. He reconsidered, adjusted his plan, created new benchmarks, and set off again. Then, another stall, so Nelson revised his approach once more. Among the new benchmarks he planned for, started toward, and then rejected were: more training, international experience, working for a boutique firm, and working for a global company. As a result of the inconstancy, Nelson's career was lurching forward (and sideways), threatening at any moment to veer into the ditch.

If you think Nelson was inept or fickle, you're wrong. He was responding to new information and feedback as he executed his plan, which is exactly right. His problem was more systemic. Every time he got more data, he reacted. But data was fully raining down on him, and chasing down every raindrop only gets you lost. He had lost the thoughtfulness of his execution.

Here's what he needed to do, which is just what you must do:

First, when new and relevant information appears, always ask: *Would this revision move me closer to my overriding goal of a great career?* Beware of a revision that is purely lateral or that only marginally advances you to the ultimate prize.

"Did your past plan revisions advance your cause?" I asked Nelson. "Or could they have, had you seen them through?"

"Well, they would have advanced my skills," he said.

"Yes, but would advancing those particular skills have made you a more desirable art director?"

Nelson thought about it for a minute before shaking his head. "No, I guess not."

When Nelson heard about a new training program, for instance, he had immediately applied, assuming it was a good thing, but without thinking of whether or not it would move him forward toward his art director goal. And then he abandoned it altogether when the exciting possibility of an international posting suddenly appeared. In effect, he was reacting to new information, not to a significantly faster pathway to his great career. Since none of the choices would have made a meaningful difference to Nelson's career, it was hardly surprising that he was bouncing around.

Now, for the second question: *If a new choice is tangibly closer to your goal, will it involve a loss of time that will reduce your advantage?*

"How long would this new training program have taken?" I asked Nelson.

"Three years."

"Three years?" I echoed. "That seems like a lot. Would it have been worth the time away from your job?"

Nelson had gained a lot of traction at work, and so no, he determined that the net affect would not have been clearly positive.

That doesn't mean that would be the case for every training program. But he should have at least asked the question before taking the trouble to apply to the program.

There was a third question Nelson also had to ask: *Will this revision limit my options?* Keep in mind that in addition to guarding his constancy of purpose, Nelson needed to guard his flexibility just as jealously. While the goal of art director working with graphic design stood unchanged, he needed as many pathways to get there as possible. So as Nelson and I discussed the training program, it turned out that it dealt with a very specific type of graphic design and might well have limited his potential pathways forward. That would have to be considered a negative indicator. Yes, the training could have been *on balance* a wise move, but the tradeoff was significant. In a slower, simpler world, this would have been a lesser challenge — but today there is very little room for speed bumps.

"It's hard to make these judgments," Nelson said, growing frustrated. "They are so nuanced."

"I agree," I said, "which is why you must be careful. The key point you need to remind yourself of is that *the effect of the revision* needs to be clear. Otherwise, stick to the plan you have."

Essentially, by asking these three questions, we're raising the bar over which a proposed revision needs to jump. In the olden days (by which I mean twenty years ago, not a hundred), there were fewer reasons for revisions and so it was less of a challenge to vet them. Today, you and Nelson face more occasions to revise. So you must be more selective about which data to react to.

The Fruitless Search for Perfection

Finally, Nelson and I had to discuss another reason he was overreacting to new developments. Nelson was afflicted with the belief that he needed a perfect plan — one that moved him toward his goal as quickly as possible and with the highest likelihood of success. So he was tempted to tinker endlessly. And every time he readjusted, he lost time — and usually for nothing. Many people do this, and they get so disheartened that they give up on planning altogether.

The problem was Nelson's belief that a perfect plan exists. I'm a strenuous advocate of career planning, as you have seen. But I did not say your goal was to never make a mistake. The only perfect plan is the one you see in retrospect. I asked Nelson to understand that there were multiple pathways to his great career. The plan he was executing, with occasional revisions, was carefully considered and would, with a high degree of probability, take him to his goal. But he'd be able to arrive there on a different planned route, too. It might be a little faster or slower, but the key issue was arriving at his destination.

So yes, plans aren't perfect, but the absence of planning sends you into the unknown. That is, after all, what separates the child from the adult: understanding that life is about mastering possibilities while staying true to your heart.

Hard Questions, Honest Answers

1. Have you determined what you will do in case of a recession or layoff? How will you adapt your plan?
2. What are your benchmarks? What is your plan for reviewing them?
3. Is your plan on track?

PART III

CONFRONTING FEARS AND EXCUSES

NINE

Anatomy of the Excuse

A GENTLEMAN WHO RUNS leadership seminars recently quoted the good Ralph Waldo Emerson to me on the subject of excuses: "Most of the shadows of this life are caused by standing in one's own sunshine." It's an apt reminder, since I see my own passion as helping my students to get out of their own way, and to help you get out of yours.

You know by now that I have had thousands of conversations about career over the years. These conversations have had starting points spanning the globe — from Hong Kong to Montreal to Los Angeles. Foremost among the many things I've learned is this: *a healthy respect for the power of the excuse.* Excuses may seem harmless enough on the surface, but they're actually like supervillains with the power to obliterate rational thought.

And so this chapter is dedicated to looking at the excuse itself — how it works, why it works, how people rely on excuses, and why. It shows that identifying and tearing excuses apart brings liberation. At the end of the chapter, rational thought should have won the day.

Excuses in Action

It's fascinating, by the way, to take a moment to watch excuses in action. They multiply like weeds. The moment I destroy the logic of a student's prevailing excuse, another pops up in its place. And then another. Then comes the great excuse of having children — an excuse so powerful I devote all of chapter 10 to dismantling it. There are elderly parents in need of care. Or perhaps a challenged child of a relative. Or "I'll be missed as a hospital volunteer." Or "I'm too old," when the person is but a young, strapping thirty-three.

"Professor, the trouble is, I really struggle with managing my time," reported a former student who was in the middle of his career.

I suggested a number of excellent time-management courses and books.

"Yes," he said, nodding seriously, "but you see, I'm really very committed to my family, and I don't want to take time away from them."

Indeed. Then his mirror image came into my office a few days later. This fellow began the conversation by telling me his familial priorities were holding him back. When we discussed how this need not be the case, he said, "Yes, but you see, I really struggle with managing my time."

This would be funny, it really would. If it were not so serious.

And then there is the very accomplished evader — let's call him Evan (as in Evan the Evader). Once the "family" excuse is done away with, Evan the Evader barely blinks before he has rebuilt and multiplied his defenses. "Changing careers would mean moving," he explains. "I'd have to rebuild a new professional network. I'd definitely need to learn to be pushier." One excuse is now three. It's a really deadly phenomenon.

Before you write me off as an out-of-touch critic, let me be clear: I get it. In the case of our accomplished evader, it is absolutely true that moving to another city can be an immense challenge. It can be expensive, disrupt relationships, or involve giving up urban conveniences or a beloved lifestyle — perhaps all of the above. In which case, these are *reasons* not to move, not *excuses.*

So what is the difference between an *excuse* and a *reason?*

If you were sitting before me in class, you might raise your hand eagerly. "A reason is factually correct, and excuses are not!"

If you were expecting ten points for Gryffindor, I'm sorry to say you'd be denied.

The fact is, most people don't make untrue or irrelevant excuses. Children do have time-intensive needs; change does involve risk; life is complicated; too heavy a workload is unhealthy.

An excuse has to be factually correct and relevant, or it has no credibility in the eyes of the person making it. This is because we design excuses to help us feel better about ourselves and our actions (or lack thereof) and to avoid blame and responsibility. And so to fool yourself, you must be very, very good. Let us recognize how great the temptation is to use excuses. It's hard to imagine a more human impulse.

So, excuses are plausible, and therein lies the problem. Once you have a plausible excuse, the debate ends. "That's that, Professor. Thanks for your attempted guidance, but as you can see, I'm stuck."

But what if it doesn't end there?

Reasons, by contrast, do not have an endpoint. They invite further thought. Reasons can be revisited if facts change. And the moment they cannot be revisited, reasons start turning into excuses. In short, a reason becomes an excuse as soon as it stops both thought and action.

Throughout the rest of this chapter, I will concentrate on some of the common excuses that can easily be dismissed (the ones that take more time get their own chapters). But I will also look under the hood of the excuse, so to speak, to examine the cultural reasons we've gotten here in the first place.

The Unknowable Future

I wear many hats, but that of fortune-teller is not one of them. I do not know your future, just as you don't know your future. I cannot say with certainty that a path will work out for you. I live in a world of evidence and logic, not magic. Even if you generated many career alternatives and evaluated them with carefully considered information, you still couldn't know for sure what the future holds for you.

But to use that as an excuse? "I don't know what's going to happen, so ... [insert shrug here]. Instead of putting all this work you're suggesting into figuring out my 'great' career, since there are no guarantees, wouldn't it make more sense to just pick a reasonable starting place and follow the trail from there? Shouldn't I just pursue *something* and hope for the best?" (It's funny how frequently we think about young people as restless risk-takers. Most that I've encountered want guarantees and certainty, and when they ask me, "I can't really ever know, can I?" they're asking the question wistfully.)

Now here's where the question of future deepens in complexity: While I maintain that there are no crystal balls, there is a little thing called *probability*. Not knowing the future is a matter of degree. For instance, it is far more probable that you will have a great career if you love your work. Your decisions have a higher probability of success if you consider more — rather than fewer — alternatives. Decisions are more likely to be wise if you are using quality information.

There is no certainty, of course, but there is greater probability. But people don't like to think about probability. They like to think about certainty, and without certainty, it's more comfortable for them to wing it than to pursue the murky, muted-tone world of probability. That may be more comfortable, but it is highly illogical. And that is the choice ahead of you: do you trust logic . . . or luck?

The Universal Excuse: Luck

Fortunately, we have a universal excuse around which we can all rally: Luck. Luck is the great leveler. Professor or dockworker, teacher or shop clerk, accountant or lawyer: who has not seen bad luck in their own failures and good luck in the successes of others? By perverse contrast, we know our achievements are the result of effort and talent, while those of others are just dumb luck.

Our reliance on luck is everywhere. Lotteries thrive. Investors and their advisors treat the stock markets of the world like great casinos, playing secret strategies that rival those at the roulette tables of Vegas. Venture capital firms invest in ten companies, hoping that one or two will be successful. The successes of Silicon Valley are celebrated, but no one ever talks about its legions of failures. Perhaps by not calculating the odds, it looks more methodical than it is. Job-seekers send out hundreds of résumés randomly, hoping that one of them will be a perfect fit.

Luck has even invaded our language and idiomatic expression.

We continue to wish each other good luck for every possible occasion, from exams to job interviews to investments. We go so far as to wish highly trained Olympic athletes good luck. Perhaps you might conclude that this incessant wishing of good luck is no more than a social convention. But conventions reflect a widespread societal belief.

Consider once again the parallel to the world of romance. There are those singles who are ready for a relationship or even marriage, but they spend much of their time hoping for it and envying the "luck" of their coupled friends. "It might just not ever happen for me," they say sadly. When friends suggest they go to an online dating site, they laugh. "That's just not how love is done," they say, and then they wax on and on about how romances used to happen. They go about their lives — going to work, going home — waiting for lightning or *luck* to strike. How utterly disempowering!

Compare this portrait — let's call her Debbie the Hopeful — with Debbie the Active. Debbie the Active wants great love and she knows it. She also knows she mustn't wait for it to come to her; she accepts that's not the way romance works anymore, if it ever did. So she puts herself in as many situations as possible that increase her probability of meeting someone she likes. If she is turned off by motorcycles but loves the outdoors, she is likely to join a hiking group rather than spend her time in dive bars. The point is, she's thoughtful about it, and she's proactive about it. It's Debbie the Active who is likely to pursue a job she loves, by the way. She's aware of the times she lives in, she doesn't just hope for a great job to come to her; she recognizes that it's up to her to find it. And the odds of her having a life that makes her happy are much, much greater than are the odds of her cohort.

Debbie the Hopeful, however, is basically just relying on luck. Hope is, of course, merely luck's more respectable brother. So we hope about every manner of subject. We hope the job works out; we hope our kids turn out right; we hope our house rises in value; we hope we do not outlive our income. There is lots of hoping, but not so much thinking. Perhaps you think this is placing too much significance on a word or two. But compare these two sentences: "I hope this works out" or "I think this should work." Listen the next time you hear either. The emotional cadence will be different. "I *hope* this works out" is speculative. "I *think* this should work" is confident.

As is probably clear by now, I fully dismiss the concept of luck. I find it insulting—to call someone "lucky" because she has a job she loves, or a strong marriage, or a winning edge is to say that she somehow didn't earn it. Only the unprepared need luck. And so as my students graduate, I never, ever wish them good luck. I wish them success instead. And you know what? They may roll their eyes at me, but they know it's liberating to have the control in their hands and not to rely on fate.

The Tyranny of Time

Of all the excuses I hear, the constraint of time is closest to a true reason. When I am told that someone doesn't have the time to consider alternatives or gather information, it is often true that, at that moment, they don't actually have the time. Of course, they had time in the past, or they will find it in the longer term. This makes the time constraint an immediate *reason* and an earlier and future *excuse*. And by the way, we all struggle for time all the time.

And then there's time as considered through an hourglass. "It's too late for me," shrugs the young man in his early thirties. He's a businessman who hates his job, he explains, and would much rather be writing screenplays or scripts for television. To get a foothold in that field, he would have had to start as an unpaid intern — something that sounds okay at twenty-two, but not at thirty-three, with a wife who is eager to buy a house and start a family.

Okay, that's one way to look at the fact that he's thirty-three. But let's see . . . he's been in the workforce for barely ten years. He will be in the workforce for another forty years. Perhaps he can't financially commit to working for free, but that doesn't mean he needs to give up and spend more years than he has so far been alive being miserable for the majority of the hours of his day. It just means he needs to follow his passion more creatively. Instead of becoming a screenwriter who follows the path others have taken, perhaps he should try in an original way that still meets his family's situation. Too late? Please! If you want to talk age, let's talk age. I'll win that argument every time, except, perhaps, with an octogenarian.

Consider Harland Sanders. In 1955, he was sixty-five years old and the proprietor of a successful restaurant in Corbin, Kentucky. Then an interstate highway came along that diverted traffic — and his customers — away. Just like that, he lost his livelihood. But he still had one killer secret recipe for fried chicken, and he went practically door to door peddling it. And so began Kentucky Fried Chicken. Colonel Sanders enjoyed nearly thirty years of success as the originator of Kentucky Fried Chicken before he died. So I'm sorry to dismiss the thirty-three-year-old who says that it's too late or that he's stuck, and yet I must.

Or consider Billie Letts. She was in her late fifties and had been raising her family and teaching college English for decades when her first book, *Where the Heart Is,* was published. She lived another twenty years as a successful novelist before dying of leukemia in her seventies.

I could go on for pages listing others who have changed course and found great success later in life, but sometimes the most effective inspiration comes from those who are older and not afraid to call an excuse out for what it is.

Heather E. was sixty-two when she wrote me that she had decided to revisit her doctoral dissertation after a hiatus of two years. "I have certainly been through all the BUT stages and the IF ONLY stages — I am so ready not to look at what stops me and only to go ahead and have a great career — of course, I am sixty-two, so it may be shorter than others', but perhaps no less important." No less important, indeed.

And sometimes liberation from the age excuse comes directly from me:

"So you believe the die is cast at twenty, do you?" I challenge. "I am several times your age — are you saying that I shouldn't try to do anything new and important myself?"

"Um . . . no, Professor."

"Good. Now let's put that stupid excuse aside, shall we?"

The Glut of Information, or Cynicism

In Part I of this book, I talked about the sheer overload that happens when you realize how many careers are possible, and how paralyzing it can feel to begin to explore them. "There would be so much to learn," says the student, "so much information to access and consider." And so I explain how to approach her search with a reasoned process. We break it down, as I explained back in chapter 3. "So much to learn" soon turns into "too much to think about."

"But Professor," they say when I call them on their unwillingness to think about one of the most important decisions in their lives, "it's impossible to separate good information from bad. The world is filled with lies, rumors, self-interested advocacy, and corrupt intent." Their interpretation of the world is all too true. But their unwillingness to try to separate the good from the bad is nothing but an unfinished argument, *an excuse*. It's the same as saying, "I don't want to be misled by false information, so I'm just going to avoid information altogether."

So you're saying it's better to be ignorant than to be mistaken? That's ludicrous. But this line of thinking happens all the time.

Disadvantaged at the Starting Gate

Excuses are incomplete arguments, and perhaps this is most noticeable when it comes to those who look like they've had the decks stacked against them from birth. For instance, having a dysfunctional family is a reason you might be insecure or shy. That explains the characteristic; but it doesn't explain why you choose not to overcome it.

What if the dysfunction was so severe that you can't get past it? Isn't that possible? Yes, it's possible — some people will try genuinely and persistently to overcome their shyness, to no avail. But because of their effort, they'll have earned the right to say they have a reason and not an excuse. Moreover, some of those who try will surprise themselves by succeeding.

Consider Lucy, whose parents were immigrants from southeast Asia. Lucy was clearly more mature, thoughtful, focused, and disciplined than her peers. She was ambitious and determined, always trying to maximize her potential. And after much effort, she was ready to achieve her career goal at a government think tank. But in the final push to get that excellent job in her grasp, she faltered. Her networking was tentative and cast her in a less than favorable light; when she met with people already working in the field, her questions were framed as apologies, not as the probing queries they were. It must have looked to them like she was networking because she had little talent, rather than that she was networking to find the best fit for her very considerable talent.

She was in fact a poor advocate for herself. Our discussion focused on this unwarranted reticence. Fortunately, with a little coaching, she articulated her problem: she was a child of her culture, a culture that cast women in a secondary role. By identifying the obstacle, she began to feel she could overcome it. Her networking conversations became more useful as she expressed her ideas more confidently. She decided she would be a free woman, free from any part of her culture that hampered her while embracing the parts that nurtured her. Her networking skills now did justice to her talent.

Or consider Mary. The deck certainly seemed stacked against Mary. She left her home country with only forty-eight hours' notice when a scholarship to attend the University of Waterloo became available. Imagine the disruption — albeit a welcome one — in her life! In her very first class, still fighting jet lag and culture shock, she listened as the professor explained that the course would be particularly challenging for first-year students, since half the class were seniors, and they would set a high grade standard. Mary looked nervously at the young man sitting next to her and asked him if he was a senior. "No," he said, "I'm a first-year, but I failed this class when I took it last term, so I'm taking it again." The student on the other side of her was a third-year student. What were the odds of her succeeding? Certainly, she was overwhelmed, and for good reason. Yet she did not make excuses, and she excelled. She looked at the deck stacked against her and kicked it over. When she graduated, employers fought over her.

The bottom line is that there are many among us facing enormous obstacles — though the two examples I've offered have been cultural, the obstacles I often hear about are of a much darker nature. There are men and women who have been physically and sexually abused. There are children whose parents waged psychological warfare against them, taking every opportunity to eviscerate their self-confidence. There are the children of pathological parents who pampered them into such a state of dependency that they are incapable of independent thought. There are children whose teachers destroyed their love of learning. And the list goes on, with horrors endured or seen that most of us cannot imagine.

A significant number of my students suffered some of the above disadvantages. These circumstances came to my attention because they chose to share a small slice of their lives with me. And not once in more than thirty years did any of these conversations end in a request for special accommodation or an easy pass. To their credit, I heard no excuses.

They got help when they asked for it, and sometimes when they did not. But help was available for *all* students, not just those who had shared confidences. So why did they tell a stranger anything about their lives, except to make him feel sorry for them? Perhaps they just wanted a stranger to know how hard they were trying, that it was harder for them than for others. It was who they were; it was their identity under construction. And they were proud.

Of the students who I knew were in these situations, almost all succeeded. No, it was not all. For some the barriers were too high to overcome; for others they were even too high to try. There were reasons. Or at least for the moment there were. I have seen too many people recover from truly desperate situations to believe that anyone is ever completely trapped with zero chance for escape. The chance might be slight and never realized, but a flicker of possibility remains.

However, by any realistic criteria, only a very small portion of the people reading these words are so disadvantaged that they've been stripped of the ability to *try* to help themselves. The vast majority of us can try, and those who do not try use excuses to avoid the attempt.

A Low Bar

Now we are getting into the deeper-rooted excuses, the excuses that may not be recognized as excuses because they seem so much like a part of who we are as a society. We don't expect to work at a job we love, and so we don't seek it. Rather, most people expect to work to make a living, preferring a decent, stable income and good working conditions. That is where the bar is. And if it's good enough for most, it should be good enough for you. This is the standard and conventional form of thinking. Know it. Be aware of it. And fight it tooth and nail, because it's all utter crap.

And as I argued in chapter 2, it simply isn't the way of the future. You can't accept the low bar because your work and the marketplace won't accept it of you.

Thirty years ago, when I was a less experienced teacher, I spoke to my classroom about the need to love their work. "Just recognize," I said, "how many times your parents come home and want to tell you about what a great day they had at work." Much to my surprise, the class burst into laughter. They thought I was making a joke, when I was being entirely serious. Either their parents told unflattering stories about work or they didn't talk about it at all—which probably meant they didn't love it. Needless to say, it was a very bad day for me, for it showed me just how low the bar is.

Another example of our poor expectations: People presume to love their work when, in reality, they do not. They love the social aspects, perhaps. Or the money. That is not the same as being passionate about the work itself. Looking forward to office birthday parties is *not* the satisfaction of accomplishment or the expression of talent. Looking forward to what you will buy with your hefty paycheck is about the payoff of work, *not* its substance. Or there are those who seem to love their work because they fear retirement. That doesn't mean they love their work — it means they love the structure it offers them!

I once spoke with an elderly person who told me that she enjoyed playing cards because it "passes the time." Passes the time before what? Death? Kill me now, I'd say! I don't ever want to look for a way to pass the time, and I don't think anyone should. I want to enjoy playing cards because I want to demolish the person I'm playing against. Why should I look just to pass the time? Let's do away with passing the time and live fully instead.

Our Culture of Excuses

It is bad enough that our human nature tempts us into excuses, but we now live in a society where excuses are close to the norm. The evasion of all responsibility is commonplace. Politicians read the polls to discover what policy to support. If it fails, it's not their responsibility — they were just following the public's guidance. If they can't get a law passed, it's their opponents' fault. The public fails to vote, using the excuse that their votes don't matter. Public servants hide in the bushes. The political process barely functions, but it is still no one's fault. No matter what happens, somebody else is always to blame or there is no one to blame.

Executives take bonuses while their companies crash. But who can blame them, because the market "turned against them" or a new technology "appeared out of nowhere." But whose job was it to foresee changes in the marketplace or in technology? And who gets fired, besides low-level employees?

Parents worry that their children are losing their way, but "it is hard to talk to them" or "they have bad friends" or "they text too much." Are those reasons, or are they excuses to avoid difficult issues?

We live in the Age of Victimization. We are all victims now. There are so many victims, in fact, it's hard to find the oppressors. And so this gluttony of excuses is not surprising. In today's stressful and highly challenging world, success in every aspect of life is hard-won. The competitive pressures of the global economy add uncertainty to our employment and sense of security. Investment returns are not assured. Technology can make an entire industry obsolete in the span of a few years. The pace of social change is so rapid as to be destabilizing. It is easy to see defeat at every turn. Thus, it is equally easy to see the lure of the excuse.

If many of us see success as uncertain, whether as an employee, spouse, or parent, then a culture of excuses is logically appealing. It is like a magical get-out-of-jail-free card. If you enable others to make excuses, you enable yourself as well. So better not criticize your colleagues too aggressively, and they will surely offer the same accommodation to you. We can all be inadequate together, comfortable that we are all alike. How's *that* for a lowered bar?

So why focus so much effort on trying to identify excuses? Because they destroy lives.

Josh, for instance, could never get anything done on time. He did complete important jobs . . . eventually. Except for his considerable talent, he would have already been fired. He was hanging on to his job by a thread. He was well aware of this issue and admitted, correctly, that his time-management skills were terrible. He had read books about how to manage his time more effectively, but their influence rarely lasted out the week.

Over the course of a day and an evening, he would start, stop, and restart projects and personal errands. And when the deadlines that he was going to miss approached, he dealt with the stress by playing video games. Instead of harping on his poor time-management skills, I told him the issue was discipline and that he had none. Since he could not control himself, he would never control, or influence, anyone else. His behavior was that of a boy, not a man. So he had better "man up" like the warriors in the games he was addicted to. Or did he really prefer pretending to be a warrior, instead of actually being one?

I cannot say this was a comfortable conversation. It wasn't. I'm sure he was pretty annoyed with me for a while. But later, after his performance and career had markedly accelerated, he told me that my comment about the game warriors was his tipping point. Through plain speaking, I had helped him look at himself honestly. And to his credit, he had. It is never my aim to strip anyone's dignity, and this isn't what I was trying to do with Josh. Rather, I see so clearly how excuses imprison people. Josh was imprisoned by the excuses he made for himself, just as Debbie the Hopeful was, just as Evan the Evader was. When you knock excuses down, one by one, you are liberated.

Now obviously, I cannot personally confront everyone reading this book with difficult questions specific to them. But if you are open to it, you can ask those questions of yourself. Or you can ask someone who knows you well and whose opinion you trust to help you see your excuses for what they are.

Sometimes the obstacle standing in your way, casting its shadow, is you. No excuses, just you. Now get out of your own way, and get to work.

Hard Questions, Honest Answers

1. What excuses do you routinely rely on? Or do you claim you have never used an excuse?
2. What role, if any, does the notion of luck play in your thinking about career?
3. What personal characteristics most stand in your way, and how do you intend to overcome them?

TEN

How Great Careers and Loving Families Go Hand in Hand

I LOVE MY FAMILY," Carly said firmly. I wasn't sure what she expected my reaction to be. Did she think I would be shocked? Did she think I'd try to talk her out of loving her family?

"What do you think I'm tempted to say?" I asked.

Carly's voice became soft. "I think you're going to tell me to choose."

She was right that she had a choice to make. But it wasn't between her work and her family.

"I want to be a good spouse," "I want to be a good parent," or even "I want to be a good friend" are far and away the most common objections I hear when I'm pushing people toward pursuing a great career. And I'm not just talking about the thirty-somethings and older. Students who are nineteen, twenty, twenty-one are already thinking over these matters. They're imagining what they want their lives to look like, and they're already worried about how to manage it all, even if they're not yet dating someone special.

It's wonderful that we value and prioritize warm human relationships. We should. But why are we so protective and defensive about that? Why must loving others mean disengaging your brain and your passion for anything else?

Great family and a great career are not mutually exclusive endeavors, and this chapter aims to make that clear. But first, a question: Is wanting a strong family life an *excuse* or a *reason* not to pursue your passion?

That depends. Many people don't want to take any sort of risk to find their passion, but nor do they want to think of themselves as lazy or afraid. And so they hide behind "family commitments." They wrap themselves in the warmth of human relationships so they can remain beyond reproach. In these cases, they are using family as an *excuse*. Their actual belief in relationships might be deep and abiding, or it might not be — that's not the point.

For others, "I love my family" is a reason. They are prepared for the thought, research, experimentation, and commitment required to achieve a great career. But they genuinely believe that great careers are so demanding of time and focus that they're incompatible with family life. Remember, reasons can and should be probed. And when we probe this reason, we see that it quickly disappears.

The rest of this chapter discusses rules to having a great career *and* a rich family or personal life, the life of your choice. Indeed, if you're careful, your great career positively enriches your family life. No, it's not easy. What worthwhile effort in life ever is? Those ready and eager to build great careers will see how to combine this ambition with their family lives, and the excuse-makers will have to find another excuse.

Rule #1: Remember the Definition of a Great Career

Popular opinion looks at powerful executives who circle the globe six times in four days and say they have a great career. Popular opinion looks at the rich traders of Wall Street, who do actually think of themselves as masters of the universe and work incessantly, and say they have a great career. Popular opinion looks at the world-renowned surgeon, saving people every day in the operating room, and say that she has a great career.

Yes, this is exaggerated, but that's what public opinion does — it makes even incredible achievements sound exponentially more impressive. What biography have you ever read about a mover and shaker that celebrated the integration of his work and family life? Usually it includes just the busy stuff that makes the reputation. "Rich and famous" appears to be the key marker of success, whether at a global scale or a community scale. That version of a great career is not what this book is about.

Let me remind you of my definition of a great career, because it is the opposite of society's view: *A career is great when it offers satisfying work, impact on the world, a dependable and adequate income, and personal freedom.*

So the first rule in building a great career is to abandon the common view of it, and recognize exactly what you are trying to achieve.

Rule #2: Let Go of Guilt

According to the Pew Research Center, 41 percent of adults say that the increase in working mothers is bad for society. Only 22 percent say it's good for society.* In short, there's a lot of guilt to go around, especially for women. I'm here to tell you to let it go. In my opinion, staying at home for the so-called benefit of your kids

---

* http://www.pewsocialtrends.org/2007/07/12/fewer-mothers-prefer-full-time-work/

does not necessarily benefit them as much as if you were working in a job or career you really love.

Now, I am certain that some readers are reacting with surprise at this perspective. But allow me to explain myself. First, the economic argument: Harvard University helmed a study of 50,000 adults in 25 countries that showed that the daughters of working mothers had more education, were more likely to be employed and in supervisory roles, and had more robust incomes than daughters of stay-at-home mothers. As for the sons, the influence there was less about career and more about the home: sons of working moms spent more time on childcare and housework as adults.[*] I call that progress.

Second, you want to be able to be a role model for your children, a role model who is happy and fulfilled, so that your kids will strive for the same thing for themselves. Please understand, I respect those who believe that their greatest passion is their family and that staying at home with young children is the best use of their time. However, for me this is a valid choice only if stay-at-home parents have carefully considered all their career alternatives and found none that approached the intensity of interest they have in their families. Otherwise, you may one day come to feel that you sacrificed your future for that of your children. I must then ask whether it is best for your kids if you become bitter or resentful about what you've missed out on for their sake?

Before you say, "Oh no, I would never show bitterness," you should know that, unfortunately, I see this kind of resentment all the time, sometimes more overtly than others. On the more extreme side, Florian from Austria wrote to tell me about a moment when he was in his twenties, and his father told him that he hadn't

---

[*] http://www.nytimes.com/2015/05/17/upshot/mounting-evidence-of-some-advantages-for-children-of-working-mothers.html?_r=0&abt=0002&abg=0

been able to pursue his career as a doctor abroad because of Florian's birth. "It is a question of how striking the moment was to me as a twenty-something-year-old, when your father, your own flesh and blood, charges you with the responsibility for his missed career," he wrote. "Back then I was overwhelmed and, in a first reaction, tried to cope with the situation by accepting what he told me . . . It is among the meanest and most unfair things you can tell a child."

The way I view it, parents do not need to sacrifice themselves, their marriages, or their careers on the altar of raising children. Doing so is counterproductive, in fact, to their children's development. By focusing only on your role as a parent, you have given up being a role model for your kids' career life. The best thing to do is to lead by example, so that you are never in the situation where your child comes to talk to you about his dream job and you think, *I had a dream once too, kid, but then you were born.*

Rule #3: Use Your Edge to Gain Control

Let's say you love your work, but your employer objects to your taking time away from the workplace. When you are at your workplace longer than you want to be, that is not a great career. (Notice we're talking about the work*place*, not the work. The work itself might still be a pleasure.)

This is a problem I see constantly — remember Betty, from chapter 4, who loved her job but felt her workload was getting out of control to the detriment of her personal life? Do what she did: Become so valuable to your employer that they accept your desire to be home more. It may not be their preferred alternative, but they agree to it nonetheless.

Married couple Ellen and Brandon both came from close-knit

families that they wished to duplicate. They wanted children, and they wanted to be hands-on parents. And therein lay the problem. They had separate career paths, and both had found work they knew they loved. But both of their chosen industries typically required long hours. For them, the hours were a deal-breaker. Both wanted ample time to be involved parents; they had rejected any choice that delegated parental responsibility to one parent alone, or to a caregiver. So what to do? They were both prepared to walk away from their chosen careers if it meant no rich family life. This meant they faced only one choice if they were not to change careers: They would have to be exceptional employees whose employers would be so afraid of losing them that they would not ask them to work long hours. They would have to be stars.

But while Ellen and Brandon were smart, they would never claim to be geniuses. So how could they be stars? Their industry norms required using brute effort to get results, but they weren't willing to do this. Instead, they conducted old-fashioned research, and each found an idea that was disruptively useful to their respective employers. Brandon found a new and expanding market for his employer; Ellen championed a new technology that dramatically lowered costs. While this path wasn't easy, it was far from impossible. Most companies, and in particular the ones Ellen and Brandon were in, rarely did such research, even as a corporate priority, and it was the last thing most of the employees would do on their own initiative. In other words, they found an edge.

By age thirty, both Ellen and Brandon had high-income jobs they loved, children, and — most precious to them — time. Their typical work week isn't more than forty hours in industries where the norm is over sixty. They both have breakfast and dinner with their kids.

Claudio, who wrote to me from Italy, was one who felt this type of life was out of reach for him. "You can't easily balance the plans for creating a good family and the plans for having a successful career," he wrote. "The people who can do both things with great results are very rare (superhumans, in my opinion), and I admire them."

I'd argue, though, that Ellen and Brandon are not superhuman. They may appear so, but only because they are all too rare. Being superhuman implies that most people could not achieve a similar balance, but that's not true. Ellen and Brandon have traits that are accessible to everyone: They are creative, resourceful, strategic, and disciplined. Anyone who loves her or his work can earn this degree of freedom. Now that doesn't mean that every situation will work out as Ellen and Brandon's did. There are bumps to navigate and decisions to make.

Stacy offers a good example of how sometimes, even when you are able to have it all, you still must make difficult choices. She had worked long hours for many years as an assistant professor in a research institution and was recently tenured. The year following gaining tenure, she was granted a one-year sabbatical, which she intended to use to do research part-time, but also to care for her two very young children. At the beginning of this sabbatical year, she was contacted by an official at a high level of government, asking her to join their team. It was a wonderful opportunity, a chance to have a fingerprint on policy that was important to her, and working for an administration she admired.

But it would also mean committing to more hours than she wanted to work, and more hours than were reasonable for her to work given the needs of her young family. Her husband was a trial lawyer at a firm with substantial billable-hours requirements, and he was up for partner that year. Their extended family was across the country. If she were to make the job offer work, she would have to hire someone to care for her children beyond normal work hours — something she didn't want — or she would have to convince her prospective employer to allow her to work part-time or reduced hours.

Stacy was a star, and surely desirable to the administration. But it became clear that the intensity of their needs would simply not match a part-time schedule. So Stacy passed. The decision was agonizing at the time, but it is one that she does not regret. She still has a job she's passionate about, but it's on her terms. Better yet, the administration still calls upon her as a consultant, and her ongoing communication with policymakers makes it very likely that she will be asked to serve again, when her children are older. Next time, she may just take it.

A poster hangs in my office that says: NATURE DOES NOT FOLLOW A SINGLE PATHWAY; NEITHER SHOULD MAN. Part of having a great career means that you can say no — to a task, to a promotion, to a relocation. A great career means that there's not just one path available to you.

Rule #4: Look for the "Win-Win," Not for the Compromise

It makes me crazy when people misconstrue my message to suggest that I am always going to side with a career opportunity when a choice must be made. If a woman moves hundreds of miles away from her child in order to pursue her dream job, I don't think that makes any sense. If a young man in love rejects his girlfriend because of a job opportunity in another country, I don't think that's wise, either.

Janet and Bentley arrived at my office in love and in need of career advice. Both were about to graduate from great programs, and Janet had already been offered a desirable job in St. Paul, Minnesota. Bentley didn't have a job offer yet, but he was confident about getting a good one, although St. Paul had a limited amount of relevant employers for him. So they came to ask about aggressive search strategies for him to compensate for the limitations of the Minnesota location.

It quickly became apparent that neither had a career strategy beyond the following: 1) get a good education, 2) get the best job possible, and 3) have a life. Janet's great job had fallen into her hands, with little thought given to it. Now it was time to apply that thought. As we discussed Bentley's search strategy, the conversation broadened and Janet mentioned casually that she'd also received a job offer from a European company, but she'd rejected it out of hand.

"Why?" I asked.

"Well, it was a smaller company," she said, "and . . ." She shrugged. That was all she really had to say.

"Maybe," I suggested, "you should reconsider and craft a plan."

It turned out that the European job had great potential and the location served Bentley's needs much better. But Janet had already accepted the other job.

"Did this company in St. Paul guarantee you a job for life?" I asked.

I needed to ask no more. Off they went to Europe, with a plan for a great adventure, and two high-potential careers.

The point is, if you want both deep human relationships and a career you love, then you need to honor both. You need to be methodical and have a plan. And you must not be thwarted by conventionality that would have you choose between black and white options.

Rule #5: Be Time-Disciplined

We've already covered how to approach it if your employer wants you to work more than is reasonable. But what if the person who's keeping you at work at all hours is you? In that case, you need to leave, and you need to have the discipline to do it.

The best vehicle for building relationships of any kind is face time. While modern communications can aid relationships, they are much less efficient than nose-to-nose conversation. That's why, even in the digital world, a video call is preferable to any kind of text. So be home more with your family. Or if you don't have kids, spend lots of time with your life partner. And if a circle of true friends is also your goal, see them often. That means time *away* from work.

Unfortunately, it's easy to lose time to work for those who love what they do. I was once told by a seriously thoughtful person that he had chosen to avoid the work he knew was his passion. "It would take over my life," he said. To avoid that risk, he had retreated to a colorless zone of mediocrity. He had in effect avoided having his life taken over by giving up his life altogether. He is the person afraid to mount a horse lest he be thrown off, and therefore he never knows what adventures he might have ridden off to. Take no risk so you can guarantee you will do nothing.

There are certainly jobs and passions that could take over your life. Entrepreneurship, for instance. Starting a company can be an exercise filled with passion, and it can also be all-consuming. But I reject the notion that it *has* to be all-consuming. In fact, if it's all-consuming, you run the risk of burning out before you achieve any results at all. The antidote to this madness is discipline.

Discipline is something I constantly work on. Economics fascinates me even more than ever, and I want to play out every teaching moment to its fullest. I could concentrate on my work literally all day, to the exclusion of all else. But I do not, mostly. I enjoy my family and personal time as much as the satisfaction I get from my work. The problem I have, as do many others who love their work, is its seductive momentum. When your mind is "in the zone" and you feel an exhilarating sense of progress, you do not want to stop. But here you demand discipline of yourself. You remind yourself that you are the master of your passion; your passion is not the master of you. You are not its puppet. (If you have never felt passion, this will make no sense. So you'll have to trust me that this is a challenge, one that you may experience for yourself one day.) As a result, the passionate people of the world must rein in their passion so it does not consume the rest of their lives.

So I make sure I take Larry time and family time. How? I just schedule it. And barring exceptional circumstances, I stick to my schedule. I want my family and friends to be able to count on me. But I sense you are making a mistake. You're assuming that I move from work time to family/friend time as if it were a zero-sum game: less work time equals more family time. But actually I'm moving among *three* choices:

1. exclusive work time, wherein I'm in my zone, writing, teaching, or meeting with students;
2. integrated work/family time, wherein my family is talking over a work dilemma with me or accompanying me to another economist's lecture; and
3. exclusive personal/family time, wherein my family and I might be on a hike or having dinner together, not discussing much of anything, but simply enjoying one another's company.

My goal is to make the integrated time grow in relative terms. In effect, I'm just using my finite time more efficiently, getting more work done, and strengthening relationships. It's like getting bonus time, and I can never get enough bonus time. And I'm not alone, since many others achieve the same degree of integration.

In the next and final rule, I will talk about the components necessary to creating an integrated work-family life. Even if you work in a hospital, or somewhere else you cannot bring outsiders, you can still involve them in your work. Read on to see how.

Rule #6: Seek Integration, not Balance

I really dislike the word *balance* when talking about careers and family. It suggests that the ideal is a perfectly even scale, with each side in its own contained space. I reject that entire image. Balance presumes that you spend your life in separate compartments labeled *life* and *work,* and you move time between them. I reject this goal. You should be trying to *integrate* your work and your life so each supports the other, making the whole stronger as a result. I know that some people say this is impossible, utterly unrealistic. To say otherwise is to admit their own failure to do so. So how do you integrate? There are two guidelines: talk about your work; and whenever possible, work together. Let's take these one at a time.

Talk to Your Kids and Your Partner about Your Work

"The last thing I want to do," people frequently say, "is to take my work home with me. I need to get away from it." This sounds suspiciously like family is the antidote to work. And if you don't love your work, that would be true. But if you do love your work, why are you trying to get away from it? Often it's because, even if you love your work, you can feel you're under exhausting pressure. And home is where you can find relaxing refuge, as you should. But remember what we learned in Parts I and II of this book: A great career does not feel like you are in a pressure cooker. If you have a great career, you're happy to talk to others about it — and doing so helps the integration we're striving for.

When I'm with people I care about, I talk about economics, teaching, technology, and the primitive state of our world, and then I ask about the other person's work. I didn't think this was controversial, but apparently it is. Once someone accused me: "You're just proving to your family that you're so self-centered you must talk about yourself all the time."

So, let's answer that charge.

In the first place, I talk about my work, not my brilliance. And I always ask about the other person's work. Of course, it's important to be age-appropriate. When kids are small, tell them funny stories and ask them detailed questions about the Lego structures they built that day. As children grow, conversations will become more involved, and you can offer each other a valuable outsider's perspective about issues related to work or studies.

But take it a step farther. Why not ask your children their opinion about how to deal with an unhappy customer? Why not ask your children if they approve of you taking a new job assignment? You might even discuss a potential investment or the purchase of a recreational property. Recognize that, apart from gaining a fresh perspective, you will get real answers about their lives.

Rose loves her work as an event planner and, not surprisingly, she is very good at it. She told me she struggles with what she calls *balance,* trying to find enough time to be with her children. I asked what she does with the precious time she does spend with her teenagers.

"Oh, all sorts of things," she said. "We take them to favorite restaurants, go hiking, go to baseball games."

"And do you discuss your work with them?"

"No," she said. "I try to keep my work and personal life separate."

"Why?" I asked. "You love your work."

Rose shrugged, "The kids would find it boring."

"Have you *tried* talking with them about it?"

"Well, no. My husband and I want the focus to be on them, not on us."

I had to be direct with Rose and tell her this made no sense to me. "Don't you want them to know who you are, who both their parents are? Don't you want your kids to know what you love and hate?" Work was a big part of who Rose was. Everyone knew that, except her children.

"Moreover," I continued, because Rose appeared to be listening, "by keeping the focus exclusively on the children, do you not notice you're putting pressure on them? These people-in-training need space to figure out who they are. Instead, you're shining the spotlight on them. Maybe you would help them find their way by letting them see yours as often and intimately as possible."

Rose was quiet for a long time, then she acknowledged she was perplexed by these ideas. I told her she wouldn't be if she could listen in on the conversations in my office for a while.

As I've said, it's shocking how many students don't even know what their parents do. When I ask, the answers range from, "I don't know" to "I'm not sure." Tom said that his dad worked at General Motors. But when pressed as to what exactly his dad did, Tom said, "Something in the office, I think." He *thinks?* Susan said her father was an engineer. She didn't know where. "It's some kind of consulting job, but I can't remember the name."

All too many of my students don't really know what work their parents do. And this isn't the fault of these young people. It's clearly the effect of parents who don't speak about their work. Do they enjoy their work? Hate it? Who knows? I used to think it must mean that they didn't enjoy their work since how could you *not* talk about that which you loved? Then I met Rose, who deliberately hid her passion. Parents often complain that their children seem like strangers. Well, of course they do. If they don't know what work you do, they don't know you — you're not sharing your whole self with them, so why would they do that with you?

Peter provided an example of an entirely different approach. His mother is a real estate developer, and his pride in her accomplishments is obvious. Moreover, in between terms at school, he works with her. "She must enjoy her work," I remarked.

"Of course," he said. Indeed, it was obvious to him. And Peter and I never once discussed the importance of passion in career success. He knew that already. Our conversations were purely about tactics to achieve goals, not the goals themselves.

The importance of talking about your work does not apply just as it concerns your children, but all people who are important in your life. Craig was an actuary who liked his work solely because it paid well, and was "sort of interesting." Unfortunately, every year the work became less interesting. So he endured his cubical life and had a drink or two in the evening to unwind; on the weekend he partied hard and drank more. His wife was concerned about the drinking, but everything else seemed fine.

Then one day he arrived home and told his wife he had quit his job. The family income had just fallen by 60 percent in twenty-four hours. "Were you laid off?" she asked.

"No." So there would be no severance pay.

"What are you going to do?" she asked, trying to keep her panic at bay.

He said he didn't know, but would take the summer to figure it out.

With a cat, dog, kid, and a big mortgage on a big house, Craig had just thrown his household into turmoil. And his wife had had no idea he was so discontent, because he never talked to her about his work.

Fortunately, Craig's wife was a saint, and she supported him as he finally found his way forward. But Craig risked more than he should have, and unreliable luck happened to save him.

Another married couple, Lisa and Derek, were a much better model. They both hated their jobs, and they complained to each other about them. In other words, *they talked to each other*. Then Lisa told Derek to stop complaining and get different training while she kept a roof over their heads. He did so, and now he has a job he enjoys. Now Lisa is back in school herself — it's her turn. And *that* is what talking about your work can accomplish.

Now back to Rose. When she expressed doubt that her kids would want to listen to her talk about her work, I pointed out that I am under siege by students and young alumni incessantly wanting to discuss careers with me. They are hungry to understand what they might do. I tell them what others have done and they listen intently. I share the lives of strangers with them because, in all too many cases, their families do not share their own stories.

Finally convinced, Rose started with a dinner with all hands on deck, and instead of asking her children the banal question, *What did you do at school today?,* she described her day at work. Amazing as it was to Rose, they seemed to listen. She planned to increase the frequency of such dialogue as much as possible.

Talk about your work, whether you love it or not. It's the blindingly obvious first step to integrating your work and your personal life.

Work with Those You Love

While talking with loved ones about your work is important, it's just the preparation for the key part of work-life integration: working *with* your family. You can talk as much as you want, but you build human solidarity on tasks accomplished, not words spoken. And so it always was, until recently. Grandparents, children, and grandchildren planted and harvested the crops; family and neighbors built the barns; the merchant's family lived over the store that they all worked in; father and brothers worked in dad's sawmill. Then, in time, everyone ran off to the city.

What kinds of tasks does the modern family work on? Every kind. The scriptwriter's children contribute trendy words and contemporary images. Dorothy and her daughter design store layouts. Taylor hunts for data for his father's reports. Martin introduces his wife to the company that will become her employer's key supplier. Anthea brings her mother's database into the twenty-first century. Gavin helps his friend find a new innovation. Jill helps her husband balance his accounts, while he helps her sell her employer's products. Leo helps his sister find financing for her business. Charles critiques his mother's business cases. Nellie rehearses her presentation in front of her children. Jim helps his son prep for college exams. Cynthia shows her son how to work a room. Sometimes money changes hands, sometimes it doesn't. One project tends to follow another. Child helps parent, brother helps sister, friend helps friend, and spouse helps spouse. How is this anything but good?

Arthur was a retired teacher who loved investing. He liked the money, but he loved the challenge of outsmarting other investors. A taciturn man, his relationship with his adult children was coolly loving and respectful. The children visited often, but mainly to see their mom. But the grandchildren changed everything. Out of the blue, Arthur asked his ten- and twelve-year-old grandsons if they wanted to learn how to invest. They both said yes, possibly because the alternative was another boring afternoon. They were hooked that first day and never looked back. Thereafter, instead of being dragged to their grandparents', they insisted on going. Barely in the house, they thundered off to their grandfather's den to spend hours in animated conversation. When the old gentleman passed on, the grandchildren, by then in their twenties, stood stony-faced with grief. They were not remembering a cuddly figure who tossed balls to them and took them to Disney World. They were mourning their partner, mentor, and teacher, the sage who prepared them for life's journey. They had lost part of themselves and carried part of him forward.

Another example of the power of work to bind a family together comes in the form of yet another funeral. Three teenaged granddaughters looked detached and distant while their grandfather's eulogy was being spoken. But when the grandfather's many workplace skills were noted, tears streamed down the faces of all three. They were remembering the things they had built together, from dollhouses to summer houses. The family builder was gone, and they knew him by what he'd built.

Perhaps you think it's depressing to comment on two funerals in a book about great careers. I can think of nothing more fitting. Remember, a great career means at the end of it and at the end of your life, you leave your mark behind. You leave your work behind to speak for you.

Do you want to know intimately the people you love, or might come to love? Talking and partying with them will get you only so far, and many people indeed get no farther than this. But when you work together with someone, you really learn who they are: what they like, what they do not, what they are good at or not, what is true and what is false.

That's how people who love their work have great careers, great families, and great personal relationships. Their work and their life merge, each both a cause and an effect, reinforcing a bond that endures.

Hard Questions, Honest Answers

1. Are you using the desire for a close family life as a reason or as an excuse not to pursue a great career?
2. Are you disciplined about how you spend your time? How could you be more so?
3. Do you talk to your family about your work?
4. Do you involve your family in your work?

ELEVEN

The Bottom Line of Great Careers

S YDNEY, A BRIGHT and charismatic student of mine, was specializing in human resources management. A scholarship student, she excelled in her studies and was in love with everything about HR. She spoke to me often about how much the challenge of nurturing, deploying, and rewarding talent fascinated her. I could easily imagine her as a powerful contributor to her organization. Then she asked a question one day that utterly perplexed me.

"I'm interviewing for a job as a quantitative analyst," she said. "Do you have thoughts about how I can use my studies to my best advantage?"

I asked her if she'd lost her passion for HR and suddenly developed a passion for the financial industry since our last meeting.

"No," she explained, "but I want to . . . consider other options." Since I want people to consider many alternatives, her answer would have been fine except for what she said next: "I'm good at math."

You noticed, didn't you, what she did *not* say? She did not say she was intrigued by how an elegant array of equations can predict the future. (That's how my quants speak of their passion.) She didn't say she wanted to explore her interest to see if it qualified as an alternative passion.

"Sydney, I'm confused," I said. "Can you explain what led to this newfound direction?"

"I'm sure it'd be an interesting job," she said, shrugging. This meant that she was *not* sure it would be interesting to *her*, since she had never set her hand to the work.

When pressed, she finally blurted out the hideous truth — the truth I suspect every time a student starts acting strangely, as Sydney was. "A friend told me how much elite analysts earn," she confessed.

Clearly, her income as an HR professional would pale in comparison. So since she was mathematically adept, why waste time on her passion when big bucks were calling? One simple conversation had made her conclude that an HR salary was a starvation wage compared to the quants serving hedge fund billionaires. She was oblivious to the difference between competence and excellence, totally disregarding the edge that passion gave to those who had loved math since before they could read. She could *do* math; her competitors *thought* in math. With the scent of money in the air, she was no longer listening to anything I said.

Now, Sydney obviously was not going to starve if she went into HR, but there are many who don't pursue their passion because they think there's no money it; and there are many who pursue something else because they (wrongly) assume there is money in it. So in this chapter, let's address the gilded elephant in the room. Let's break down our assumptions about money-rich and money-poor careers so "I would pursue my passion, but I will starve" will no longer work as an excuse.

Money Matters

Sydney had convinced herself to give up her passion in order to follow the money, but in many cases, my students have been pressured to let go of their dreams by their parents. I'm sorry if that sounds harsh, but it happens to be true. We want our children to do well, to prosper. Money matters. Financial security matters. But the usual advice about how to get money and security is entirely wrong. For instance, consider the parent who spoke to a career counselor and asked what the difference was between the starting salaries of actuaries and accountants.

"Both are very well paid," replied the counselor.

"But exactly what is the difference?" insisted the parent, who then explained, "My child is going to choose the one with the highest income." Where was the child in this discussion? Did it matter? He was apparently going to do what he was told. This kind of conversation plays out in similar ways all the time.

Then there was the soft voice of a high school student who had applied to a computer science program and had not yet received an offer. "Have I been turned down? Should I send more information? I really, really want to do this," she added. And she called every day, with the same almost-begging tone. Once or twice, another voice could be heard in the background. Then suddenly, the applicant asked, in an almost hushed tone: "I have just one question — what do computer scientists do?" Obviously, her parent had left the room.

Where exactly does this over-involvement and pressure come

from? It's only by understanding its roots that we can find an answer. The problem is that our society tends to have a schizophrenic view of income. While most people have "average" incomes, they simultaneously wonder why their income isn't higher while worrying that their income might fall to a much lower level. These dual concerns are neither surprising nor inappropriate. But all this anxiety has a great cost: *the loss of careful thought.*

So let's bring careful thought back.

Let's look at three categories of jobs in a careful, critical way. The first category of jobs are the Gold-Plated Jobs, like the one Sydney was attracted to. These are the jobs that seem safe and well paid. We'll break this category down, though, so the gold-plating disappears and you can see what's underneath. Only by doing so can you effectively challenge the assumption of the seemingly great career that your parents or your peers are steering you toward. With the Gold-Plated Job shown for what *it* is, you begin to see the "risky" options for what *they* are . . . which is not necessarily so risky.

Which brings us to the second category of jobs, the jobs that make parents quiver with fear. These are the jobs like actor, artist, athlete, and astronaut — although they can also include jobs in the upper echelons of anything (as long as it begins with an *a*, apparently). These Scary Jobs seem like long shots to get, but the upside of success is great indeed. This category takes up the lion's share of this chapter, for these are the jobs I most want to strip of the fear they inspire.

Finally, there's a category of jobs with no apparent prospect of employment. These are the Outlandish Jobs, the jobs that make people laugh, perhaps, when you tell them what you're interested in doing. These are the jobs that, if you pull them off, people are fascinated. These are the jobs that convince people that anything is possible.

Gold-Plated Jobs (High Income/Reasonable Chance of Employment)

You might be thinking, *If a career has a high income and a reasonable chance of employment, what is the prof's problem with it?*

Well, first, don't assume I have a problem with it. Fields with relatively high incomes, like finance and technology, often do have a reasonable number of job openings. It's still competitive to get hired, but the number of entrants is limited because the educational requirements are stringent. There might actually be great need in these areas, or a limited pool of new entrants because the job is thought of as unattractive, like some of the skilled trades. And some of them come with extremely high pay.

I now just heard a collective sigh of relief from a legion of students and their anxious parents. Sorry, but you should have kept holding your breath. I *did not* say there was a plentiful supply of great *careers*. Or did you forget that a good income is only one of the criteria of a great career?

Indeed, some of the jobs in these high-income fields *might* be great careers, or they might not be. So what's wrong with many of them?

Narrow Range + Volatility = Disaster

First off, in the vaulted tech and finance industries, the jobs with strong demand cover a relatively narrow range. Not every engineer faces multiple job offers. Not every job in finance is in demand or even pays particularly well. Don't assume that just because you get your MBA, you will get a consulting job at McKinsey.

But still the hype surrounding the tech and finance worlds mesmerizes many people, who unnecessarily limit their search for the elusive good jobs and the even rarer great careers. And then they complain to me they cannot find their passion.

There's so much they don't consider. For instance, since many of these jobs are based on narrow specializations, as someone grows in their job, that person's capability actually narrows and is less mobile. The finance guy who specializes in subprime mortgage securitization is a well-respected expert. But what happens when that market emphasis is replaced by something like forward hedging for foreign currency transactions? How is he to use his expertise then?

Such a narrow focus *might* be tolerable if you knew that the narrow specialization would be in demand at your employer and every other similar employer for all your life. But you don't know that. You can't.

My student Jackson was sure he had an answer to that problem. A techie who had never met a trend he didn't love, he practiced what he was pleased to call "agile employment." First he specialized in enterprise management software, and when that passed its peak, he moved on to e-commerce; when that became routine, he headed for cloud computing. He always earned a salary bonus for a few years, and as soon as his earnings plateaued, he put his hand to the Next Big Thing. He was proud of his "modern" approach to career. With everyone and everything on the cloud, Jackson then rushed to data mining, where his plan fell apart.

He entered the data-mining job market with no sustaining specialization, just his well-established record of adaptability. But he then slammed into the graduating classes of mathies who reveled in all the mysteries of data mining. Their new knowledge dwarfed his, and the guy who interviewed him was younger than Jackson. Jackson was suddenly yesterday's man, at just thirty-three. The person who bounced into my office when he was a student now arrived almost somber for our conversation.

The underlying challenge in these particular high-profile, trend-setting industries is their high volatility. A twitch in the financial markets can hurl thousands back into the job market in less than a year, as happened in the financial meltdown of 2008. And a new technology can destabilize entire industries in months. So while there are reasonable prospects with respect to hiring and salary in many positions in these industries, the career potential is not great unless you can withstand the disruptions, ideally by instigating them. In short, Jackson's way was doomed to fail. Even in the midst of rapid change, Jackson had forgotten to take it into account. Most of us do not like the consequences of rapid change; but trying to ignore change does not help.

Lifestyle of Constant Work

These Gold-Plated Industries are notorious for their punishing, long hours. The reactions to this brutal regime vary. There are those who revel in the demands with a fourteen-year-old's macho mentality. ("I don't eat, I don't sleep, I don't have a life, I code.") Others are so blissed out they brag to me that in their excellent job, they have wonderful free food, showers, massages, foosball, Friday beer, and dry-cleaning services.

Certainly, there are many perks, presented as a demonstration of how much the employer values you . . . with the entirely accidental effect of keeping you in the office far into the night. (*Why leave? You have everything you need here!* Put that way, it's uncomfortably like "Hotel California," isn't it?) I recall one young man who bought a sports car with his signing bonus. When I asked him how he was enjoying it, he said that every weekend, he went to the parking garage to look at it. There was, of course, no time to actually drive it.

Why do these very well-educated people tolerate such long hours? The answer is simple. Whether by intention or not, workers in both tech and finance are being played just like rubes in Vegas. A very few young people in a few prominent companies make abnormal financial gains, even become wealthy. This is often because they are early employees of a company that goes public, or they worked at and partly owned a company that was bought by a megacorporation. Or in the financial industry, some receive bonuses that exceed their annual salaries. In other words, they struck it rich, and they are celebrated endlessly.

Just as the winners in Las Vegas are given lavish public attention, the effect is the same: hold out promise to the army of players who will not win a huge amount in order to keep them at the tables or the machines for as long as possible. Slot machine or computing machine, is there much of a difference? Keep turning out the deals and you too will get a massive bonus; keep coding and your stock options will buy you a private plane.

Even though these Gold-Plated Jobs have never applied to more than a relative handful of people, they have created a powerful standard against which everyone, including Sydney, now sets themselves. No matter how abnormal, it becomes the goal to aspire to. And you may be assured that your friends will be in awe of your financial success, should you get the prize. Forget the long hours, lightning might hit. As every gambler has vowed, if you're not in the game, you can't win.

Scary Jobs (High Income/Risky Chance of Employment)

Kelly wanted to be a novelist, and she spent every free moment imagining her characters and plotting her books. But she didn't have a lot of free moments, as writing was not her career; she was an academic advisor at a small college. She often wondered if she should just quit her job, devote herself to writing for a year, and see what happened. Perhaps she would break through and become the next J. K. Rowling. The other alternative was to focus a week or two of vacation each year to her writing, but she figured it would take a decade to make any inroads. She felt that quitting her job was the only way she could make meaningful progress. Kelly is the classic example of "I would pursue my passion . . . but I will starve." No, you won't, Kelly. *If* you have a plan.

I'll get back to Kelly in a moment, but first let's be economists for a moment and break down this category of job for what it is and why it is that way. The jobs that may offer high income and poor employment prospects do so for one of two reasons. First, the quantity of new entrants in the field is very high, swamping the number of new jobs available. For every final roster of an NFL football team, there are thousands who seriously tried and didn't make the cut. For every novel accepted by a publisher, there are thousands that were rejected. For every headshot singled out by a casting director, thousands were discarded. While some people do succeed, and in a big way, for most of the people in these fields, the average income is low and erratic.

The second reason some of these careers are so ostensibly out of reach is that the number of job openings is minuscule, so low that, even with a small pool of incoming applicants, some will inevitably be left unemployed. If you want to be an astrophysicist or marine scientist, you may wait for years before someone retires and leaves a job open.

Though these obstacles are very real, neither of them eliminates the Scary Job as a possibility. In Kelly's case, she has many more choices than she can see. She's afraid that using her vacations for writing won't get her where she really wants to be, but she doesn't have a plan for how to make those breaks move her work effectively and quickly to her goal.

For example, Kelly could adopt interim goals: get a short story published in a literary journal, win awards, gain a commission, or find paid writing work, even if she wasn't writing novels. And yes, for a short time she should blend this activity with her job at the college. The goal is to prepare her career as a writer so that, when she's ready, she can quit today's job and move to her passion.

I don't agree that it would take a decade part-time instead of a year full-time. A year full-time without a plan is just a wild gamble that might or might not work. Many artists struggle for years full-time without real success. Most of them are just rolling the dice and trusting their fate to luck.

The Worthy Effort

Having a plan does not guarantee success, but it does guarantee a fair effort. From the time Colin was a child, he had wanted to be a professional soccer player and had worked at it aggressively. He worked out, trained, paid for specialized coaching, and achieved amateur ranking.

But try as he might, he couldn't get an offer from a professional team. And for his sport, he was starting to get old. Colin felt it would soon be time to put aside this particular passion. Having exhausted all his possible options, he was right. Indeed, Colin's behavior was exemplary: determined, patient, and aggressively exploring alternative pathways. But just because you pursue a considered goal persistently does not mean you will succeed in the end. No, we do not always live happily ever after. So the question is, did Colin do the right thing by pursuing a soccer career so vigorously?

What is the actual choice facing those who feel they have a true passion? Too often, it seems like you should either resolutely persist until you exhaust yourself, or give up before you start.

"Don't give up! You must at least try!"

Is that what you think I'd say? You'd be wrong. I've met too many people trying to enter crowded fields who are destined to fail, and I'm not just talking about athletes. For those almost sure to fail, I would say, "Don't waste your time trying."

Of course, I would say *more* than just that.

I would say, "Don't enter a crowded field unless you're prepared — really prepared — to minimize the competitive pressure in that field. If you merely accept that the field is crowded and you decide to do no more than try, you face a high likelihood of being bitterly disappointed." As I've said before, it's *everyone's* strategy to try, and to work hard. The truth is, you need to do better than that.

Colin understood this. He knew he needed to separate himself from the pack, and not just by being vaguely better. He identified the key attributes of successful soccer players and found, not surprisingly, each had a distinctive strength, something they could do that most other players could not. Some were more agile, others had superior speed. Others could see multiple plays unfolding in real time. Others seemed always to know what the other player was going to do before the player himself knew.

Colin looked for such a distinction in himself, and tried to train for his own special, rarely seen competitive edge. He was right to do so, and I was right to encourage him to try. He was by no means doomed to fail. But as an athlete, the frailties of the human body gave him a narrow time frame in which to succeed. His failure was honorable, because his attempt was well conceived. Unfortunately, the same cannot be said for the many who try without any realistic hope for success.

The Artist's Block

While Colin was doing everything he could to succeed, Carolyn was initially her own worst enemy. She was a visual artist who did not need to be an international sensation. But she did want to earn a decent livelihood doing the work she loved. Many of the artists she knew barely survived on their art alone; one sold real estate to pay the rent. Similar situations face many of those in dramatic and artistic endeavors. On some occasions, they lament their lack of income as evidence of the degeneracy of the world. On other occasions, they play martyr to their art.

When Carolyn asked for guidance, I began by discussing ways to improve the marketing of her work. I asked about her artistic distinction, her edge, what new value she was bringing to the world of art. She did indeed have a good answer, believing that works of trompe l'oeil were much undervalued. She wanted to use that technique to explore images of the contemporary world. I commented that this had good possibilities.

Then she looked worried. "If I create salable work," she said, "I fear I'll be compromising my artistic integrity."

"Oh?" I asked. "Why is that?"

"There's this gallery nearby," she explained, "And they're great, but they actually sell art with a two-week return window." I gave her a puzzled expression, so she continued. "A *return* window, as if artwork was a pair of jeans. The gallery says it's in case the buyer finds that the newly purchased work clashes with the room décor. I'm an *artist*," she insisted, "not an interior decorator."

I take integrity very seriously, as should everyone. After all, in the last chapter I challenged us all to be true to ourselves. So I took Carolyn seriously, which permitted me to ask her more questions. "Does artistic integrity mean that you don't care what others think?" Implicit in my question was: was her vision of integrity simply an assertion that she was the center of the universe?

Carolyn didn't want to say this, but she hadn't thought about integrity in that context. If she wanted to make a living at her passion, she needed to see herself in the context of what others would pay for her work. For many in the artistic and performing worlds, this is a radical thought.

Carolyn came back after some time and a lot of reflection. "Okay, Professor," she said. "I don't think a marketing plan will sully my reputation too much."

Once she had implemented her plan, sales of her work accelerated, as did her prices. And what big compromise did she make for money? She reduced the scale of her work to make sure it could actually fit into the homes of her likely buyers!

Then there was Lester, who was determined to be an actor. I asked what his plan was.

"I'm not going to get discouraged," he said. "I'm going to just try and keep trying."

"That's a personality characteristic — and a good one — but it's not a plan," I corrected him.

"I have a list, too, Professor, of every possible part I could try to audition for."

"A list isn't a plan, Lester. Are there priorities on your list? Are the possibilities categorized between warm leads and cold ones? How do your acting strengths apply to each particular production?"

"I'll act in anything," he said. "I don't have a choice." But again I insisted that a list is not a plan.

"I'm an artist," he said, "and artists don't need plans. I just have to be persistent, and with —" He stopped himself and I raised my eyebrows.

"Luck?" I offered.

He bowed his head, not acquiescing, for he knows I would have shouted at him. But he had closed the door nonetheless.

I never did persuade Lester to develop a real career plan. Even though he knew how competitive it was to get even a minor part in a thirty-second commercial, he could not bring himself to recognize that the more intense the competition, the more aggressive the plan needs to be. While career planning is not common in most fields, those in the creative or artistic fields seem to be positively hostile to it. Lester and Carolyn are not unusual in this regard.

However, this means that the odds against success in these artistic and creative jobs are not as high as they appear. Since many people pursuing these areas are making multiple mistakes, like Lester, that almost guarantee their failure, those who plan carefully have a distinct advantage. Again and again, I've been privileged to watch talented men and women enter these domains where the number of competitors is high and the chance of employment low. But they have succeeded across the wide range of creative and artistic jobs, from photographer to filmmaker, from writer to producer, from narrator to actor, from movie reviewer to animation artist. All of them minimized mistakes, developed an effective plan, and worked their plans aggressively.

Being Aggressively Creative

Now, back to Colin before the suspense kills you. A professional soccer career wouldn't work for Colin, but he had a backup plan—an alternative passion, and not just a default occupation to make a buck. (You can see why I liked Colin.) He wanted to be a paleontologist and had already taken preparatory courses to confirm this fascination.

Unfortunately, his research had told him it was a long educational process culminating in a PhD, and then most positions were at academic institutions. While there wasn't exactly a mob of students entering the field, jobs were not plentiful. So he'd have to be very good to succeed, and he wouldn't know whether he was good until he had invested a considerable amount of time. He had already concluded he was not quite good enough to be a pro soccer player — *what if this were true again?*

Before further discussing paleontology, I asked if he had any other strong interests. "I like watching clouds. I could watch them all day," he replied. "And don't tell me to be a meteorologist. I hate weather." (I have found that when you have strong views about matters, people have a tendency to tell you what you're going to say next.)

Colin could be forgiven for thinking that the world was out to get him. As it turned out, Colin had been afflicted with *both* aspects of poor career prospects; with soccer, there was a high number of applicants; with paleontology, there were few positions ever available.

"If you're to get one of the scarce jobs in paleontology," I said, "you'll have to be very good. So, what's your plan?"

"Work hard?" he suggested. "Or, um, or maybe not . . ." he added, as I looked unhappy.

"Perhaps add a touch more creativity," I suggested.

"Right now my main concern is getting the grades for grad school. What does a creative approach have to do with that?"

"It doesn't have to do with the grades," I explained (patiently, I believe), "but it has everything to do with the marketability of your degrees. Your education should have two purposes: To develop your competence as a paleontologist, and to get you your job. Just being competent, and being certified as competent, does not get you your job, which is especially true in a field where there are few openings."

We brainstormed for a bit longer, and I reminded him that in any credible graduate degree, there is a required piece of research.

"So I should use my creativity there?" he asked.

I shrugged. "Some graduate research is simply another way for the student to practice their skills, and a significant result is not expected. As a result, students lose a valuable tool to secure competitive advantage."

"So I should try to solve a research problem creatively?" Colin asked.

"Yes, you could," I noted, "but even more importantly, you should be *strategically* creative."

Colin almost glared at me, with the student's typical just-tell-me-the-answer look on his face. But I'm a prof, and my job is not to answer questions; it is to make my student smarter. And my reader, too.

"Since jobs are scarce in your field," I said, "wouldn't it be a good idea to find out what the biggest, most important questions are in paleontology and focus your research on them? Shouldn't you find out what important research problem is being investigated by the museums with the largest paleo exhibits? Since most of your competing student colleagues don't think of doing this, just as you didn't, *that* is where your advantage lies."

"But wouldn't this work take longer than just banging out the degree?"

"Yes, but I thought you had a work ethic."

"Touché," Colin said, and I was relieved to see that he grinned. "But if I choose a difficult problem, maybe I won't be able to solve it."

"Yes, that's a risk. But if you've identified a truly important problem, or a practical chunk of one, in the right schools, this alone recommends you for admission. But," I admitted, "this is aggressively creative; creatively find and shape an important problem and then creatively solve enough of it to mark you off from your peers. It's easier than you suppose, since most don't even try. This means the bar of success is lowered and therefore within reach."

"If I stretch," Colin said.

Exactly.

Outlandish Jobs (With No Employment Prospects)

Colin was entering a field with relatively few jobs, but imagine you have a passion that doesn't even fit a defined occupation. In other words, the world has told you it will not pay for what might be, at best, your hobby. So what do you do? Abandon this passion and find another one? Maybe. But before you do that, you should try to find out if you can persuade the world that you offer enough value to be paid. Of course, if you don't have a well-considered plan for how to make that argument, you had best move on, since the odds of success are remote.

Nevertheless, I have watched people turn the most unlikely passions into paying careers. I know of a guy who left doodles everywhere he went. He now designs corporate logos. What about the person who ran a successful business selling parts for obsolete phones? (There happens to be a large market of people who restore old phones. Who knew? The people fascinated by the history and elegance of old technology knew, that's who.)

A former student of mine, Bartosz, is the general manager of the Snow School at the world-class ski resort Whistler Blackcomb in Canada. He wrote, "I was an engineering student for almost three years at Waterloo when I decided to take your Econ 101 class . . . Long story short, I dropped out of engineering to pursue my pas-

sion for skiing, of all things. I still needed a degree and after trying for three terms, they accepted me into the Recreation Department. Well, the rest I will not bore you with, but . . . *I have a great
career!*"

Miranda loved knitting and had an eye for design. What do you
suppose she did? Do you think she knit little baby booties to sell
at the local flea market to urban moms who wouldn't pay more
than four bucks for them? Someone without a plan might, merely
to cover part of the cost of what was no more than a hobby. But if
you have a true passion, and you are organized and thoughtful, you
might take an entirely different approach.

Miranda, in fact, was not a regular at her local flea market. She
launched a North American scale endeavor that included speaking,
teaching at workshops, and publishing lavishly illustrated knitting
books. Who bought the books and attended the workshops? *Those
who shared her passion.*

The lesson here is twofold. If you want to make a living at an unusual activity, you need to connect with those who share your passion, whether for knitting, skiing, or old phones. Or you find those
who would pay for your service only once every ten years, like the
logo designer. They have no need for a logo artist on their payroll,
but they will pay for the service. Find enough of them and you have
a business.

And that represents the second lesson. Most of these opportunities are "created" occupations, exercises in entrepreneurship.
This is hardly a new idea: if no one hires you, you hire yourself.
The passion comes first, and then you "package" it so the world
can use it, keeping in mind that there are lots of kinds of packages.
If your passion is not connected to an occupation, you need to consider whether you are ready for the life of an entrepreneur. If you
aren't, then you search for another passion.

The Virtue of Flexibility

Let me share two final stories about people pursuing their "risky" passions. Joe wanted to be an actor, and he had learned to be both disciplined and flexible. He had a detailed plan, but he was also open to taking different kinds of jobs. The result was that he came to see his passion more broadly — it wasn't just acting but the entire entertainment industry with which he was engrossed. So he worked in — and loved — a variety of roles, from stage manager to producer/developer, to talent manager.

And then there's Dakota, an administrator for a large private company who was attracted to a position as coordinator for a nonprofit that worked with the elderly. But she was reluctant to pursue the job because it paid so much less than her current job, and she wasn't sure she could make ends meet. Her thinking about the problem was the same as so many of the people you've met throughout this chapter, from Kelly, who imagined she had just options a and b, to Carolyn, who was sure she must choose between selling out and selling high art. It's never that simple. *There is never just one way, position, situation, or employer.* Look resourcefully and creatively for your passion *and* a decent income. Dakota needed to find a way to use her talents in the service of the elderly that also would allow her a lifestyle she loved — a lobbying job, perhaps, or a position with the government. The point is, there is never just one job.

Finally, unless you can get your desire for, and misconceptions about, financial gain under control, you are forever disadvantaged. If you vibrate between greed for as much money as you can make and the fear of having nothing at all, your mental machinery will misfire. Of course you should want to secure a decent income. But you cannot let the lure of money either distract or blind you.

Hard Questions, Honest Answers

1. What assumptions do you hold about money and career?
2. How are you being strategically creative to make your great career financially viable?
3. Are you truly open-minded and flexible about how you might work in your field?

TWELVE

When Your Passion Collides with Your Fears

T HIS CHAPTER IS NOT meant to erase fear from your life. I couldn't do that even if I wanted to — it's just unrealistic. Besides, fear is too useful for me to *want* to do that. Let me state the obvious: we do not want to live in a world of fearless people. Fearless people start wars. Fearless entrepreneurs go bankrupt and waste enormous amounts of time and treasure. Fearless children ride their bikes without a helmet. So I don't want you or me to be fearless. Fear is good. Fear protects us. But we must not let it paralyze us.

I believe that fear should always be treated with the greatest respect, never batted away or dismissed like an inconvenient pest. Everyone has been afraid at one point or another, whether they admit it or not. And often, they've been afraid for good reason — there's much to be afraid of in our world, even if you don't make a habit of watching the six o'clock news. There are many legitimate reasons why we might fear for our family, our health, and our economic well-being. There are also phantoms that bedevil us needlessly. The trick is in figuring out which threats are real and which are not.

Sebastian was beset by fears on all sides. When we met, he was struggling both academically and in regard to his career. He was torn between different career alternatives, and he could think of many reasons why each of them might end in disaster. One of them — hotel management — seemed a candidate for real passion, but he refused to consider it carefully enough to know. He was effectively paralyzed with fear. I asked him to tell me why he was afraid to commit to a plan of action.

"It's just who I am," Sebastian replied instantly. Then he added, "And don't tell me to be brave. I don't have it in me."

But I had no intention of telling him any such thing.

Or do you think I should have?

The truth is, fear cannot be so easily dismissed. If a few words would do it, we'd live in the land of the brave. To pat him on the back and say something like, "Sebastian, my boy — be brave! You can do this!" would have been to treat him as if he were a child being coaxed into the deep end of a swimming pool. Or worse, it would have implied that I thought he was weak or really did lack courage. And that would have been profoundly disrespectful. So I did not tell Sebastian to be brave. But I did tell him that I thought he was mistaken in some of his assumptions. It makes for less dramatic dialogue, but it's also more powerful for being true.

I asked Sebastian to try and understand his fear. What you understand better, you can then take the first step to manage. And when you can manage your fear, you can take actions you would not have otherwise considered. This is not bravery; it's *reason*.

In this chapter, we'll look at some of the most common issues driving fear. I'm sure you'll see ways to identify and to examine your own fears, and strategies you can use to move forward.

The Fear of Wasted Time

"Sebastian," I began, "what would happen if you pursued an education in hotel management, and decided it wasn't for you?"

"I would have wasted too much time — at least a couple of years," he said glumly.

"Would that entire time have been wasted?" I asked. "Would you have not learned anything useful?"

"Well, maybe I'd have learned a few things."

"And what might you have learned?"

"I might understand a few things about financing," he said.

"Nothing else?" I pressed. As you can see, this was a painfully slow process as, step by step, I got him to reflect upon and acknowledge the various skills he'd learn. We went on like this for a while, then Sebastian struck the mother lode.

"I'd learn how to keep hotel guests happy and willing to return again," he said.

"Yes," I said. "And what else would those lessons apply to?"

Now Sebastian saw the potential, as his brain leapt over its barrier and clicked into high speed. His fear had distracted him from thinking. I had, in turn, distracted him from his fear. And he was now able to recognize that learning how to satisfy customers in the demanding hotel environment was highly applicable to a wide range of other service industries, from insurance to travel to retail.

Even if Sebastian ultimately decided hotel management wasn't for him, in such a course of study he would learn a highly mobile and important skill. He would also acquire some knowledge of financing, marketing, and personnel management. And any competently taught hotel management program would include networking events, so Sebastian would be able to add to his potential mobility by building his personal network. Sebastian already knew that the scale of this network added to his employability.

In other words, when he examined his specific fear — wasting precious time — he found it would be much less of a waste than he had casually assumed. As a matter of fact, the danger was much lower than he had supposed. While it took a lot of conversation between the two of us to get there, Sebastian saw how a hotel management program could realistically help him become successful. There was still uncertainty, but it was about the degree of the success, not the intensity of the danger. Sebastian took action and enrolled. Was he still anxious? Yes, but he was now managing the fear and moving ahead.

Fear of wasting time is pervasive. And Sebastian was right to take the threat seriously. After all, you have only so many years of life. A year, once wasted, is gone forever.

"Professor," my students object when I say dramatic-sounding things like this, "you're making it worse! I'm already scared enough!"

But the entire point of this discussion is that understanding your fear must be based on the truth and a full consideration of the truth. Otherwise, if you never confront your fears, you'll never know what you could actually have accomplished in your life.

Those who justifiably do not wish to waste time need to do whatever they can to save it instead. For instance, Ophelia was determined to try to become a fashion designer, but she knew it was risky. So she wanted to devote the shortest possible time to her attempt; if she failed, the time she'd have lost would be minimal. With guidance from established professionals, Ophelia discovered the most efficient way to test the marketability of her designs. Putting her shingle up on the Internet, for instance, was not the way to do it. It could take years for her to break through that way, or even to gauge if she had the necessary talent. Rather, she needed to get feedback from a strategic cadre of buyers at select boutiques, which she did by building a team and getting key introductions. As it turned out, her test was successful. But even had she failed, she would have learned something from the experience, and in the shortest amount of time possible. In sum, efficiency is a beautiful thing, and it girds us against the fear of wasted time.

The Fear of Missed Opportunities

There's one more way to reduce the threat of wasted time, and it also assuages the fear of missed opportunities. In clichéd terms, strive to kill two birds with one stone. In the more specific sense, make each of your actions serve many purposes. It's a bit like multitasking turned on its head — how many objectives can you accomplish in the course of a single meeting or class? Allow me to explain.

Winston realized he needed to pursue this dual route, as he was passionate about both financial analysis and high-level computer-game design. While he had a job in the financial industry, he feared that if he continued with that and did not pursue game design, he would never know if he had chosen the better of the two. But if he tried to do both in sequence, he worried that such an approach would take far too long. His fear of wasting time was mixed up with his fear of missing his best opportunity.

"Why not pursue analysis and game design at once?" I asked.

"Because if I don't focus, I'll make a mess of both," he said.

Really? Well, by now I'm quite good at noticing conventional thinking, and this statement was obvious. "So you're going to just make that assumption," I said, "without even thinking about how you might do both at once?"

Winston didn't consider himself a conventional thinker, so I suggested that, at the very least, he create a plan to see what might be possible. He would have to find actions, I said, that advanced both purposes at the same time. It took some effort, but when he thought carefully and creatively, a whole new set of possibilities opened before him. Indeed, Winston became a fan of "parallel processing." For example, at a networking event, he discussed whichever of his interests seemed appropriate with different people at the event. Winston also noticed that some were even interested in both his ideas. He had two separate elevator pitches ready, of course. When he attended a conference on new financial instruments, he wondered how he could apply those principles to game design. When he attended game-design conferences, which he did on his own time, he speculated about whether any of the suggested strategies could be applied to the design of financial instruments. As he followed his parallel pathways, he discovered more and more of these double-barreled opportunities. He imagined roles he might play in game design that would actually utilize his financial-instrument skills as a great asset. The two could work together to give him a great edge.

"Are you drawn more to one than the other?" I asked when next we met.

"No," he said. "In fact, both are becoming more interesting than ever." Doing them simultaneously wasn't just efficient, he explained, it was downright exhilarating. "I feel like my brain is firing on all cylinders." Winston also confided that he now understood the real danger he should have feared: that by wrongly choosing one pathway or the other, he would have missed doing both. "That thought really scares me," he reflected, "even though it's not what happened."

I myself am an aggressive practitioner of parallel processing. I am passionate about architecture, for instance. If I go to an economics-related event in a different city, I often take the opportunity to tour the city's famous buildings. For years, I'd read and learned about economic difficulties surrounding architecture. Then I realized that architecture students were not signing up for economics courses on their own, and yet the economics of architecture is critical to their professional development. So I had a meeting with the head of the architecture school and suggested teaching an occasional class on the economics of architecture, which I've been doing for years now. Economics, teaching, and architecture, all in one. Not all career areas are broad enough to bring in so many other disciplines, of course, but you see the potential.

In my case and in Winston's, parallel processing offered opportunities to combine dual passions. But for others, parallel processing confirms that one choice is better than another. Great! Now they could proceed without second thoughts or regrets. They tried both, and on their own learned which career was better for them.

Parallel processing is a challenging approach, one that requires planning and research. But it doesn't require courage or overcoming fear, just determination.

Fear of the Unknown

Another common fear, which is often hard to describe, is the fear of the unknown. That is, you don't know you're afraid of it because you don't know what you don't know — and that itself is the fear. Are you confused yet? Stay with me.

Paula was the junior manager of a retail operation, a position she hated. So she researched management roles that she thought she might find more interesting. Project management looked promising, and there was a clear educational and career pathway. But what if she did all the work and ended up performing poorly as a project manager?

When we broke it down, it was clear Paula was a confident young woman. She had many logical arguments to make about why she would probably do well as a project manager. But she was still afraid, and her fears were holding her back. Why?

Together we considered a number of obstacles, none of which seemed to apply. For example, she wasn't overly concerned about wasting time or missing opportunities. She didn't seem to lack confidence in her abilities or in her learning potential. Even though she had a job she disliked, she delivered acceptable work on time.

"Why is it that you think you'll fail to perform in work you would most likely enjoy?" I pressed.

"I don't know!" she said, exasperated. She couldn't define her fear — she just knew she had it, and that it was preventing her from taking action.

It was time to play detective. We needed to really unpack what it meant to be a project manager and see if we could discern which part of it made Paula so uncomfortable.

I asked Paula to walk me through a typical project-management assignment, step by step. Paula described the process well, since she'd done her homework. It took her only a few minutes to take me through what an entire project would look like. And that was exactly the problem. She had only *read* about project management, so of course she was uneasy. Paula had no actual, concrete knowledge of the work. It was all academic, not emotionally understood. Remember that balance between emotion and logic we went over in Part I? She didn't have both in equal supply, and so she needed to speak with those who did the work. She needed to hear someone who loved project management tell her why he did. If what he said didn't resonate, Paula might then conclude it wasn't the best choice for her after all.

Paula's fear, once pinpointed, was very real and very valid. She was right to be afraid of the unknown aspects of her choice. The good news was that she could address those concerns and then make an informed choice without the heavy baggage of fear influencing her.

Over the years, I've been surprised at how many times the anxieties of my students are based on limited information about a career. They're right to be afraid, but they're often not doing anything to correct that deficiency. Instead, they spend their time trying to talk themselves into overcoming their fear. They say things like "I'm trying to be a risk-taker," or "I've just got to man up and take the plunge." They spend too much time reacting to their feelings, or talking about them, and too little time thinking about why they have them.

By all means, get in touch with your feelings. Just don't get distracted or obsessed by them.

The Fear of Ambition

Like Paula, Trudy was bedeviled by fears that she had great difficulty articulating. If I may wear my Sherlock Holmes hat for a bit, I will admit that this case had me stumped. Trudy was emphatic that she'd found her passion. She loved being an electrician. She was already licensed and well regarded by her employer. But she really wanted to run her own subcontracting company. This choice would combine both her love of electrical technology and her fascination with enterprise. But Trudy couldn't bring herself to launch her business.

"Are you afraid of going bankrupt?" I asked.

"No," she said. "My initial investment would be relatively small, and if the venture fails, I can go back to my current job."

"Are you sure?" I pressed. "You're not concerned you might not get your old job back?"

"No," she said confidently. "There's a lot of demand for my experience."

"Are you worried your reputation with your family or friends might take a hit if you fail?"

"Definitely not," she said. "They'll be impressed that I at least tried."

I was running out of possibilities. "Are you afraid of disappointing yourself?"

She hesitated. "Perhaps," she allowed. But upon reflection, she said, "No, that's not it, either."

Maybe you think that Trudy is in denial? But her answers were very clear, very reasoned. Unfortunately, this discussion about failure was not helping and seemed to be making it less likely she would launch her enterprise.

I remembered she said that her family and friends would be impressed she had tried. Maybe there was more to that statement. Was she afraid of flying too close to the sun, as the mythological Greek character Icarus had?

"Trudy," I said, "Do you know anyone who's started a business? I mean, personally?"

"Come to think of it, I don't. Why?"

This struck a chord. If she didn't know anyone who had started their own company, that would lead to a real fear; after all, she had no role models. That would be a challenge for anyone. Moreover, she was a woman in a nontraditional field, and she was raising the stakes by starting a business in the construction subtrades. It would have been a miracle if she had not been uneasy. I suppose I could have given her a speech about female empowerment to encourage her. But that would merely be using one emotion to battle another emotion—it would be no different than telling her male counterpart to act like a man, and that, as you have seen, is beside the point.

Instead, I suggested something much more to the point. Her problem was that she didn't have role models, so she should try to find one. She should talk to the owners of other subtrade contractors. She did so, and she met several who were the first in their families to start a business. One was even happy to serve as her mentor. None happened to be a woman, but now she saw others like her, from similar backgrounds. Her ambition no longer seemed a stretch. She launched her business. She was still nervous, but she'd defeated her hesitation. She'd defeated the fear of ambition.

Fear of Failure

Of all the many fears I help my students diagnose, fear of failure is the most common. And sometimes it's seen in people from whom you'd never expect it.

Sam received an excellent job offer in a field that fascinated him — microbiology. The job was even located in a city where he wanted to live. So when he came to see me about the details of the job offer, I thought our meeting would be primarily celebratory. But then our discussion circled around some minor issues in the offer, and it became all too clear that Sam *wanted* to find something wrong with it. Then he could turn it down in good conscience.

When I suggested this possibility to Sam, he didn't deny it. Instead he said, simply, "I'm afraid I'll screw it up."

As it turned out, his prospective employer has a very high profile, and that had caused Sam to almost panic. Objectively, there was little reason for his apprehension. He was a top-ranked scholar, with relevant experience for his would-be employer. But such objective reasoning offered little psychological comfort.

I took Sam's fear seriously, and we set about trying to figure out why he was afraid of failing. I knew Sam was part of a close-knit family, and he was their pride and joy. Perhaps that was the source of his anxiety.

"Are you concerned about disappointing them?" I asked.

"Of course," he said.

"Does anyone else in your family have a graduate degree?"

"No," he replied, "no one has any kind of degree."

"And do you think these facts might be related to your reluctance to take an excellent job?" I said. "Perhaps to avoid any chance of disappointing your family, you want to take a less demanding job?" Note that this is not some amateur-hour pop psychology. These are just logical questions about career choices and family circumstances. And I have asked them many times.

Sam didn't agree with me right away. But he did say he would think about my questions.

When I next heard from Sam, he told me he had taken the job. He justified his choice by noting that, even if his family had never found out about the offer, he would be disappointing them by failing to take it. Does that sound like it was too easy a way for Sam to deflect his fear? Maybe, but in my experience, I have found that sometimes a single question or observation sets off a train of thought that leads to a remarkable result. Sam was one such example.

Roxanne's fear of failure was more difficult to diagnose. When she came to see me, she had a job she loved — she was a gifted designer with a track record of accomplishments behind her. But her career had stalled. She didn't get the most recent promotion she'd applied for, and she'd recently received only a modest performance review, not in keeping with her past success. Roxanne brought the review with her when she came to talk.

Her supervisor had given her a rating of "acceptable" performance, and had commented that she needed to stop selecting work "beneath" her. Roxanne explained that her company liked its designers to pick which new design projects they wanted to work on. These preferences were accommodated whenever possible, with the more experienced designers having priority in the selection of work. Roxanne's boss was criticizing her, as one of the more experienced designers, for picking the most routine new projects. Her choices meant the less-experienced designers were left to tackle the more challenging projects.

"Is that true?" I asked. "Do you do that?"

"Yes, probably," she said.

"Why would you pick the more routine projects? They must be less interesting."

She shrugged. "I like them."

But that's the kind of answer you would expect from someone who doesn't love their work. Those who love their craft typically want to stretch and challenge themselves. "Have you lost interest in design, Roxanne?"

"No, not at all!" she said. "It's more interesting to me than ever."

"Can you explain?" I asked. "It's very confusing to me that you would pass on the more demanding projects, and the chance to challenge yourself."

After a bit of hesitation, finally she said that she knew she could always produce a great design on the more routine projects — the ones she'd built her reputation on. They were safe.

Roxanne was afraid of failure, but in a different way than Sam. She didn't think she would fail to produce a *good* design; she was afraid she would not produce a *great* design. As a young employee, she'd been uneasy about achieving excellence in her work. But she had, and along the way she'd discovered a profound sense of accomplishment. She didn't want to put that glorious feeling at risk by leaving her comfort zone. In short, she'd become a prisoner of her own success. This is not an easy trap to escape from.

I asked the obvious question. "Can't you just slowly tackle the harder projects? Don't take them all on at once, but just little by little? That way, you can slowly add to your reputation while minimizing risk?"

Roxanne looked grim. "I could have done that. I *should* have done that. But it's too late now. There are rumors that the design studio's being 'rationalized'—I think there might be layoffs coming. I have to do something quickly to protect my job."

Roxanne was in an all-too-typical situation: she'd tried to avoid an immediate danger and had increased her likelihood of a future with greater danger. She had to face that greater danger now.

She felt she needed to select the most difficult problem offered by her employer and hope for the best. But Roxanne seemed so anxious that her abilities could well have been impaired. Still, there was some good news for her.

"Roxanne," I said, "let me ask you something: do all the other designers at your company have your degree of passion?"

"One does, for sure," she said. Then she thought for a bit. "For the others, it's just a job, I think."

"So consider this: in the design department, you really just have one competitor, only one person who over time could match your performance."

Roxanne hadn't thought of that before. It provided some reassurance as she went back to work to tackle the toughest project she could, and it helped her manage her fear of failure.

I learned later that Roxanne had fared well with the harder project she took on, and survived the layoffs. But she would be the first to acknowledge that it was a close call, and one that could have been avoided, had she asked herself what we all must: Am I fearful of stretching myself because my comfort zone is just so . . .

comfortable? Am I fearful of risking the failure that can come with real growth?

The Fear of Financial Distress

Even with a solid plan, even with a clear deconstruction of career strategies, even with role models and a brain full of information, fear of the unknown can stop you — particularly when it comes to financial matters.

Interestingly, I've found that this fear of financial distress isn't just present for those who want to be actors or painters, but even for those who intend to pursue relatively well-established careers with good salaries.

Let's say a product developer — someone who designs toys, for example — doesn't take a job in a small company, even though the work is exciting to him, and opts for more generic work in a bigger company. I see this circumstance all the time. When I object (as you know I do), the typical response is either: 1) "There's more security in a big company," or 2) "The pay is higher." Sometimes I get both responses.

Again, we must attack conventional thinking, for both of those responses are unfounded. Big companies have reorgs and layoffs all the time — just because they've been around for years doesn't mean that you will be around with them for years. And the pay is only higher if you look at it through a very short-term lens.

Fear distracts from rational thought, and sometimes it takes a while to determine the root of the anxiety. My student Foster, for instance, seemed adamant that he would sacrifice much of his passion to maximize his immediate income. Foster was an engineer. When I asked him why he would give up his passion in this way, he plainly said he was afraid of being poor.

"There's a big gap between being poor and maximizing your income," I pointed out. In other words, he need not take the six-figure job that he knew would make him miserable just to stave off homelessness.

"Yes, but the farther away from poverty I am, the safer I am," he argued, quite logically. "Then if something goes wrong, I'll have resources to survive."

Like all of my students, Foster had heard me say that rising competition was forcing people to follow their passions for great careers. He agreed with me about rising competition. But he concluded that the best way to protect himself from its rigors was to stockpile as much money as possible while he could. It's not an uncommon conclusion. It's my argument turned on its head. And you may be tempted to agree.

But Foster was wrong, for one very simple reason. His argument was logical only if applied to the immediate future. If he failed to pursue his particular passion in engineering, he was destined to become a commodity engineer, easily outsourced, or even replaced by a well-trained technician. In the long term, pursuing his passion, not immediate income, would best secure his employment and earning power. I reminded him that he'd already heard this argument.

Foster didn't react well. "You're trying to scare me," he said. Then he added, "You don't understand how scary poverty is to the child of an immigrant family."

Then he stopped and grew very quiet. Indeed, he was too smart not to notice that he had criticized me for two mutually exclusive failings. Was I trying to scare him or just minimize his fear of poverty? Actually, neither. I was simply trying to get him to understand his fear of financial distress and why he was moving toward it, rather than away from it.

"Foster," I finally said. "Listen to me. I am worrying about the next fifty years of your life, even though I won't live to see most of those years. You, on the other hand, are worrying about the next couple of years, even though you *will* actually live through those fifty years."

"Okay, Professor," he said. "I'll think about that."

That's all I could ask of him, or of you—think about it! I don't know what Foster ended up doing, but I hope he hears me still when he feels the fear of financial distress. Naturally, I also left him with plenty of fearsome cautionary tales to help make my point. I told him about John, from chapter 1. Remember him? He's the fellow who had the great house, and the safe, seemingly stable job at a large and growing tech company. John was interested enough in his work, but he was not really passionate, so he was surprised to be laid off as a 9-to-5er. Sure, he had done well for a few years, but his long-term earning potential took a huge hit. Remember Jake, also from chapter 1, who was laid off from good job after good job until he decided to pursue his passion for travel and became a timeshare salesperson? Then and only then, as you may recall, did he thrive. There's only so much you can stockpile in the short term, and there's a hopefully long life ahead. And you should know that I am writing this book not just for you, but also for your grandchildren. The best way to fight fear of financial distress is to take the long view.

Fear of the Fog

The most difficult type of fear to address is the kind that cannot be defined or pinned down. You can only begin to understand fear when you move from a sense of generalized anxiety to the specific reasons for it. The more exact you can be when describing your fear, the easier it is to understand. Vague fear is like a fog, hard to see through, and capable of bringing everything to a halt. The answer seems simple, right? Define your fears, and just shine a light. But it's easier said than done.

Keith suffered from this particular challenge. He was sure he'd love to work as a police investigator. He was already experienced in security and had undertaken police training. But he couldn't bring himself to actually apply. Together we went through a wide range of possibilities concerning his reluctance. Was it fear for his personal safety? His reputation? His effectiveness?

All three were concerns, but they weren't the reasons that were holding him back. Was it that he didn't know enough about the job from those who'd done it? No, not that either. He'd already talked to officers about their work and felt well informed. We were both at a loss. But if you eliminate everything else, then what's left must be the answer. (Another page from the book of Sherlock Holmes, of whom you may have guessed I am a fan.) If Keith didn't have a specific, significant fear, then the weight of the minor concerns taken *together* must have been holding him back. But then, how to deflect the fear? Simple: We would fight Keith's generalized fear with another, even greater fear.

The Greater Fear

As you have seen, there are several effective ways to respond to fear when you understand its source and nature. But if all else fails, there's one approach that almost always works. It's not a substitute for the other approaches, but should you need to pull it out, do so.

Keith faced what are in effect two fears. First, there was the generalized fear surrounding police work. The second fear was the one I showed him. "If you turn your back on policing," I said, "you'll be forgoing what looks like the best use of your talent, as well as the satisfaction it would bring." Keith had to make a choice: he could fear those issues directly associated with policing, or he could fear what he'd lose out on by not pursuing his passion. One or the other fear had to be faced down, and only he could determine which was the greater.

I did not push him beyond presenting him with his choice, but I'm happy to report that Keith is indeed a police officer today. And our world is safer for it.

There could be many combinations of fears at play, as there were for Keith. Some must weigh the fear of immediate job loss against the fear of future job loss. Some face the fear of a small financial loss versus a greater one. Some weigh the fear of failing at a small accomplishment against the fear of failing at a major accomplishment. In most of these situations, we naturally tend to fear the immediate danger and discount the future one. But in the arena of career, the future cannot be sidelined. This book is not about simply getting a job; it's about being happy and fulfilled over your lifetime.

This should be the greatest fear for all of us: failing to achieve the highest use of our talent. In my case, I was afraid I could not conquer my shyness, afraid I was out of my depth and circumstance. But I decided that one fear trumped the others. I was more afraid that I would waste my talent and energy on second-best alternatives than I was afraid of failing. So I used that fear to overcome the obstacles.

In other words, fear the consequences of the path *not* taken. If it is the path that should have been taken and was not, the cost is high indeed.

Fear as an Excuse ... or Not

As I said at the beginning of this chapter, I believe that fear should be treated with great respect, for it's usually quite genuine. But fears can also easily morph into excuses. When the impulse of fear arises, examine it, understand it, and probe it for ways to overcome it. Resist the strong temptation to use fear to avoid both thought and action. Thinking about fear is itself anxiety-inducing, and action takes effort — fear is often a convenient justification to avoid such aggravation. All the time, I see people accept their fears by shrugging and saying, "I am who I am," as Sebastian tried to do, and then retreating into apparently safer territory.

We should without exception try to specify and understand the fears we will all inevitably face. But for some of us, our fears cannot be addressed with logic, evidence, and thought. Fears in such instances arise from complex reasons or unknown sources. In these cases, professional help should be sought as soon as it's apparent that the fear has become debilitating and you cannot understand it yourself. Some fears are a reflection of mental illness. If you think this might be the case, please seek help immediately. There are many treatment options.

I get emails from all over the world where people describe their fears to me. They use words like *paralyzed, terrified,* and *afraid.* Fear is very real, and I would never say to these people, "Toughen up! Get over it!" To really battle your foe, to make your fear a helpful resource instead of a debilitating force, you must first understand it. You must unmask it. It's a powerful process to put fear in its proper place — a place that will serve you. So take fear seriously, and examine it well.

Hard Questions, Honest Answers

1. What are you most afraid of? Or do you claim you have never been afraid?
2. What happens when you examine that fear?

CONCLUSION: TAKING ACTION

You have read more than a few stories in this book about other people's career struggles. (And if you have another several hours, I could fill them with many more. I have hundreds of examples available.) But reading and studying will only take you so far; there comes a time when you must take action. Using the questions I've asked you throughout the book, you should have honed your own course of action. Don't stop when you've read the last page. There is much to do. Continue taking action. Continue moving forward.

This book is about *talent:* how to find, nurture, and use it. Yes, it speaks of careers and jobs, networking and interviews, innovation and pitches. But this is all in the interest of realizing your talent. Everyone reading this book has a talent. Your talent is more than skill and knowledge, more than the sum of your experience. Your talent will mobilize all you know, have done, and can do for a single purpose: *accomplishment.* Driven by your passion, your talent will deliver accomplishments you care about. And, most important of all, your talent will feed on itself, with each accomplishment being stronger than the one before.

I am well aware that many still believe that the preceding words are hollow. *Actually,* they think, *all we really want is a decent job for good pay. And on the weekend, that's when we will enjoy life.* But my experience with thousands of students over the years tells me a very different story. Most people do not know what a great career looks like or have any idea how to achieve it. But as soon as they are shown what is possible and what others have done, most will dramatically reconsider their choices. Most people see a far greater range of choices than they did before. It is encouraging—I myself was very encouraged. Until I saw what happened next, time and again.

Many of these people saw their pathways to great careers, but they hesitated. In retrospect, I guess I shouldn't have been surprised. We live in a world that doesn't encourage great careers, except in empty rhetoric. Family and friends offer little practical advice, just the usual platitudes: *get a safe job, work hard, and your dreams will come true.*

Sadly, this kind of cautionary conventional thinking can be paralyzing.

For the hesitant, I watched as career excuses erupted in a virtual avalanche. Thought and effort were avoided, and the easy pathway was transformed into the only apparent road left: get a safe job. How convenient.

It is unfortunate to miss your true vocation because you did not know such a choice existed. But it is a real tragedy to find the pathway that will lead to great accomplishment and then turn your back on it. Even worse, you will know you did this, and the "what-if" question may haunt you to the end of your days.

Another group lies at the opposite end of the spectrum of the hesitant. This group is mesmerized by their passion, to the exclusion of all else. They plunge ahead without any real conscious thought or plan. The wreckage that usually results merely serves to reinforce the caution of the uneasy. And even more talent is lost.

Thus, the fund of humanity's talent erodes as individuals achieve less than they could, and we are all the poorer for it.

I know I've recommended a challenging course of action in this book. I've told you that a great career is not *only* about passion or education or skill or experience. Each of these is essential, as is a well-researched, carefully crafted plan. It is not easy, and it is certainly not quick. It can be frustrating, and steps must, on occasion, be retraced. But the bottom line is that it works, as an army of former students have told me.

I understand that I've suggested a range of actions that can feel intimidating, if not overwhelming. I have been in this game for a long time, but I sometimes feel overwhelmed myself with the complexity of great careers in a rapidly changing world. One relief for this overload is the support of those closest to you, and yet many of my students don't have a clue how to get it. As young and not-so-young people try to work these ideas through their heads and decide whether and how to take action, they often ask me how they can explain a "surprising" choice to their family or friends. And it sometimes seems they are unsure of how to explain the choice to themselves. Let me suggest how you might tell your family, partner, and friends about your career choices.

What Shall I Tell My Family?

Over the years, many people have told me about their career plans, often wrapped up in the goals for their lives. They speak passionately and articulately. Even when they are unsure about their future, they can usually explain the source of their uncertainty. I sometimes need to let them speak for a while as they circle the idea they want to express. And on other occasions, I need to ask questions to get the heart of the matter. These dialogues are very important to me, honored as I am that almost-strangers are sharing intimate details of their dreams.

Unfortunately, I am often told that their parents are adamantly opposed to their proposed career paths. Sometimes there is anger on the student's behalf, and other times sadness. Of course, if they're talking to me, it's probably because they don't feel they can talk honestly with their families, so it's not surprising that they often speak of their families in an unflattering way. If some parents heard what confidences their children shared with me and not with them, they would be heartbroken. I know I would be if that happened to me.

So if you are a parent, and if you happen to be peeking through this book the way some parents eavesdrop on my conversations with their kids, I ask you on behalf of the thousands of children I have taught: Please listen. Please let them finish what they want to say. Make clear by your actions that listening to them is not just waiting for your turn to speak. Remember what you know to be true: even if they did foolishly immature things when they were fifteen, they are grown now. You must treat them with true respect, or you will not get respect in return. And do not be misled by the appearance of respect. Some of your children are good actors.

If you are the child, do not think you are without fault. Often you will tell me the detailed reasons why you want to pursue a certain career, reasons that clearly demonstrate both maturity and thoughtfulness. Then I ask you if you took the time to tell your family your plans in as much detail as you told me. The young often tell me "not exactly." That of course means they did not, and some have the grace to look slightly embarrassed.

And do not tell me your family doesn't listen. Perhaps they don't. Then ask explicitly that they do. Communicate! Admit that for most of your life, if your parents said *Do X,* you said *No* on principle. Admit that, many times in the past, you asserted your right to do what you wanted without debate. So you are not used to making a reasoned argument, and they are not used to hearing one from you. Accept you might have to work to establish your own credibility. Take the time and make the effort. If that effort fails, as it might, you'll know that at least you tried. And the fault won't be with you.

However, you also need to remember that dialogue is a two-way exchange. If your family objects to something you said, listen to their reasons why. If they don't explain their thinking, ask them to. Keep in mind a bizarre possibility: *they may actually be right.* You might be mistaken about some aspect of the career you're intending to pursue. If so, you need to know that. Recognize that this book has asked you to undertake many steps to achieve a great career. While doing your homework, you should have generated a powerful argument to justify your choice. That was the whole purpose: to make an informed decision that covers all the issues. So you should have the substance you need to justify your planned course of action.

This dialogue might take some time. You're discussing your life, so it's a serious matter. And serious matters are not discussed over a rushed breakfast or at the tail end of a casual discussion about the laundry, when your parent is distracted. Yes, the distraction strategy may have worked when you wanted your curfew relaxed, but this is not kid stuff. If you want to be listened to and taken seriously, you have to act grown-up. So make sure your career conversations are conducted without time constraints or buzzing phones.

If you're the child of a family advocating a cautious, conservative career choice, recognize why they might be doing so. Did your parents suffer great disadvantage in the past? Are they still frightened by what happened to them, and they don't want that to happen to you? Respect that concern and talk about it. Don't let it be the unacknowledged topic in the conversation, the topic that derails the dialogue. If you're the child of an immigrant family that took great risk to leave a familiar place to resettle in a foreign land, recognize the sacrifice that your family made for your benefit. Of course, you are at liberty to point out their inconsistent position: that they want you to take no risk, even as they took a major risk. If your parent is pressuring you to take over the family business, recognize that it means a great deal to that parent to see their business endeavor span generations.

Let your parents know that their sacrifices and care have not gone unnoticed. Help them understand that they raised a smart, thoughtful, and brave kid. Help them accept that you are now ready to take responsibility for yourself and your destiny. Ask them for their continuing love and support.

I fully understand why any thoughtful parent wants only the best for his child, and here I will speak to that eavesdropping parent again: You want your child to be happy and safe. You want to know that this will be true long after you have left the stage. But recognize that if you push an obsolete or unwanted career choice on your child, if you insist they take actions that once worked but no longer do, you put your child at the very risk that you want them to avoid. They cannot just pursue the path you chose, and these are no longer the days of your early life. Guard yourself against conventional ideas that you and your friends share but that you have not examined in years. Do not so easily assume that your children are being disloyal to you; they are merely trying to be true to themselves. If you force your children into careers for which they are unsuited, I beg you to understand that you may damage them more than you can imagine.

Please understand that grades in school do not tell you what your child is suited for, what they will thrive at, or what will make them happy. I am one of those who assigns such grades, and I know for sure the grade is no more than a single piece of momentary data, sometimes accurate and sometimes not, sometimes of significance and sometimes not.

In your heart, you know this to be true: *when your child is using his talent to its fullest, he is most likely to be both happy and successful.*

What Shall I Tell My Spouse?

Difficult conversations about career can also occur between spouses. They're usually initiated, often suddenly, by a spouse who wants to make a major career change. A transfer, promotion, or a return to school may be involved. Or other times, the spouse can no longer tolerate his or her current work and just wants out by whatever means necessary.

Changing careers is disruptive in the best of circumstances. Talking about it with a spouse or partner is particularly fraught because of how intertwined your lives are; the choice may have an adverse effect on your spouse's time or the family's finances. A promotion might mean a heavier workload and more pressure on your partner to manage every other aspect of family life, including childcare. A transfer can involve a longer commute and less family time, or it might be as disruptive as a move to another city.

If you're planning to disrupt your family by accepting a transfer, and you are doing so solely for financial gain, then you should note how much extra money the family will have. Of course, in that case you will have to hope that your spouse values money more than happiness. However, you might be taking a promotion because you enjoy your work. Now you need to explain why the disruption in your family's life is worth it.

You might start by emphasizing the importance to you and to the family of having everyone pursue work or studies they enjoy. Reiterate to your spouse that you would equally support him or her for an equivalent reason. Make explicit why this new position is so much in line with your goals for a great career. (If you do that carefully, you might come to conclude that your present position is just as satisfying. If so, then why move?) Discuss how you will jointly moderate the disruptive effect of the promotion or transfer. In short, ask explicitly for the other's support. You can't just casually assume that their support will automatically be there.

In addition to counseling people about their promotions, I also see many older people who want to make a big and maybe risky change in order to find or secure work they love. They are eager to make this change because for years they chose to work for money, status, security, or glamour, and slowly the work has ground them down. So now what?

The conversation you want to avoid is the sudden one, but I see these happen all the time. In this scenario, the spouse who can no longer stand his work quits suddenly and without speaking to his partner beforehand. This can be especially distressing, since it causes family income to fall sharply, leaving one person to carry most of the financial load, at least temporarily.

There are no perfect words to say in such situations. But first, you might apologize for not telling your spouse sooner that your work was becoming intolerable. Explain how you felt it was affecting your health or sense of well-being. And also be ready to explain what you want to do now, in detail. Otherwise, you will look like you took this step capriciously. Describe the plan you have come up with to find a much happier position for yourself. Ask for your spouse's suggestions for your *joint* plan. Ask for patience since this transition may take some time.

What Shall I Tell My Friends?

Friends are highly influential forces in our lives, and we should never forget that. In some cases, their influence rivals or exceeds that of family, and, indeed, adult children may spend much more time with their friends than with their families. Unless the pull of the family is very strong, young adults will soon be captured by a crew of their own contemporaries, a circle of friends that is short on experience and long on influence. Moreover, the young are notoriously affected by popular culture and its norms. Again and again, I've seen my students struggle at least as much with their friends as with their families.

Think not? What do you suppose the reaction of friends will be when one of their group receives a job offer from a huge and powerful company and turns it down to go to grad school? Or turns it down because it doesn't appeal to her, or it doesn't fit his career goals? "Are you crazy?" is the most common response. Conventional thinking is never more powerful than among friends who see each other frequently, where the message to conform is ever present: go for the money, go for the security, go for the power. And a little glamour is a bonus. So what should you tell your friends when you choose to pursue a great career and some of your steps apparently sound "stupid" to them?

Explain your decisions and goals. No, you do not *have* to, but the support of friends for the challenges ahead is not to be dismissed and can be just as valuable as the support of your family. Your explanation can parallel what you would share with your family, with two exceptions: First, you can be more insistent than would be appropriate in most families. Second, instead of trying to persuade them that you are right, explain to them why they are wrong. Try to help them understand that *their approach is putting their careers* at risk. Explain the risks in our hypercompetitive economy. Such efforts may not work, but you are right to try.

This may take time and practice. You may not have a lot of practice discussing substantive issues with either family or friends. (Sports outcomes, computer-game strategies, and romantic hypothesizing do not count as serious conversation.) Nevertheless, there are three outcomes of these conversations that make the effort worthwhile: First, your friends might agree with you and alter their own career plans. Second, they might reject your arguments and you will notice all the flaws they make in theirs; they might easily dismiss evidence, hold on to their conventional ideas without real justification, repeat the same assertions as if somehow repetition revealed truth, and even exhibit a lack of thoughtfulness. Third, you might find yourself struggling to address their points. You might not have good answers to their questions or concerns, in which case, consider that an indication that you should go back and reconsider your decision. As I have argued throughout this book, you must take great care in choosing how to pursue a great career. Mistakes can happen, and strong debate with your friends can either lead you away from danger or confirm your own judgment.

What Shall I Tell Myself?

The greatest benefit of having to justify your choice to others is that you come to fully understand your own choice. Since you have chosen to follow your passion and undertake the difficult work of creating a great career, you are walking against the tide of contemporary society. Do not for one minute underestimate how powerful that opposing force will be. It will try to wear you down, distract, and delay you. You therefore need to remind yourself of both your goals and the steps you are taking to achieve them. And you certainly need to explain to yourself why you can expect to succeed. Since you are pursuing a radical idea, your mind has to turn the idea over and over, to explore it from every angle. Fundamentally, your mind needs to get comfortable with its radical choice. And the more you think about it, the more you will get used to that choice.

You need to have a thorough dialogue with yourself in which you confirm the identification of your passion. Remind yourself that you cannot stop thinking about it and its implications. Discuss with yourself all the relevant alternatives. Review all your research to make sure you are well armed with accurate information. Review your plan. And face down your anxiety, even your fear. Ask yourself what exactly you are afraid of.

Remind yourself that there are two distinct alternatives before you, whether you want to recognize them or not. Unless you take the above steps, you will drift to the path of least resistance, where some or all of your talent will be wasted. The other pathway, however, leads to a great career. There is no middle path.

Since a great career is your destination, wrap your mind around what it will be like. See yourself eager to go to work. Feel yourself deeply satisfied with the product of your work, proud of what you have crafted. Appreciate the impact you will have on your chosen part of the world. Imagine that you have taken your talent as far and as high as you can. Imagine a life well spent. Imagine that.

ACKNOWLEDGMENTS

Any worthwhile accomplishment is always easier when you can draw on the support and talent of others. And I am deeply grateful to all those who helped in the crafting of this work. The support and encouragement of my family, immediate and extended, has been invaluable, as always. I owe a special debt to Carly Watters, my literary agent, who had to persuade me that this was a worthwhile project. Both of my editors, Kate Cassaday and Rick Wolff, provided wise counsel, and we delivered a better book because of it. I am also very appreciative of those who agreed to be quoted in the book. Finally, my collaborator, Jenna Land Free, played an indispensable role by helping me in so many different ways to give voice to this message.

Preparing Your Plan

Now that you have a snapshot of what a plan might look like, it's time to begin making your own. Let's look at what we covered in Part II in step-by-step form. But instead of thinking about Heather, Trent, Ricardo, Yolanda, Bart, or anyone else, consider your own way forward. If your pad and pencil or laptop are not at the ready, I must ask, why not?

Your Plan

Step 1: Determine the Destination

- What are your goals for your life?
- What are your goals for your career?
- Are you being precise, yet not pinpointing?

Step 2: Distinguish Your Priorities

- Which of your goals are the most important to you?
- Which are the least important to you?
- Are there any goals you could defer for a time? (There is no right or wrong answer.)

Step 3: Identify the Specific Barriers to Achieving Your Goals

- What are the real obstacles to achieving your goals? Don't fear them, just list them.

Step 4: Probe the Barriers and Revise Your Goals if Necessary

- How are others finding their way around obstacles?
- Are any of your goals adjustable?
- Are you trying to fit your passion into a conventional job description?
- Are there ways to fast-track a prohibitively long process?

Step 5: Identify, Acquire, and Strengthen the Skills You Need

- What skills do you need?
- What, other than going back to school, can you do to build skill?
- Have you determined how your skills can be continuously improved?

Step 6: Put Your Team in Place

- What are the parameters of your network?
- Who is on your team? How are you utilizing your team?
- Do you have a two-way relationship with your team members?

Step 7: Find Your Edge

- What are you doing that no one else is?
- Can you identify and solve an important problem?
- Can you use a tool or technique that no one else is using?

Step 8: Sell Yourself by Selling Your Idea

- How are you going to market your ideas?
- What is your elevator pitch?
- What is your first paragraph?
- What is your one-pager?

Step 9: Execute and Revise

- What are your benchmarks?
- Do you have set intervals at which to review your benchmarks?
- If you make a revision to your plan, are you sure it will move you closer to your overriding goal?
- Are you sure the time it will take to execute the plan will be worth the benefit?
- Are you certain your plan won't unnecessarily limit your options?

INDEX